Cooking and Preserving Vegetables

Colour Library of Step by Step Cookery

Cooking and Preserving Vegetables

Translated and adapted by Marie-Christine Comte
With an introduction by Gill Edden

ORBIS BOOKS·LONDON

Contents

© Istituto Geografico De Agostini, Novara 1974
English edition © Orbis Publishing Limited, London 1974
Photographs by Paola Martini
Recipes adapted from l'Unil-It, SpA
ISBN 0 85613 174 1
Printed in Italy by IGDA, Novara

Foreword

One of the marks of good cooks is the way they use basic ingredients to produce varied, interesting and nutritive menus. Those who follow the recipes and information in this book will find many ways of using vegetables, both familiar and strange, so that family and guests can eat well at all times of the year. With modern methods of packaging and transport you are rarely tied to purely local, seasonal produce, but even with foreign supplies available there are times when what you can buy is limited by prices. The serving suggestions here, some economical, others more extravagant, should spark the imagination even in the depths of winter.

Cheese, too, is a basic ingredient that can bring life and variety to a menu. Eaten just as it comes, with crusty bread or a biscuit, it makes a satisfying lunch or a good addition to a dinner party. Cooked cheese dishes can make a super luncheon or supper dish fit to offer to your most discerning guests.

The Colour Library of Step by Step Cookery will cover the whole range of good cooking. Each book is complete in itself and together they take you from the start of a meal to the end. In them we describe the preparation of dishes with the greatest care and include plenty of detailed information about the foods used, their nutritional values and how to make the best of them. You will find few short cuts — our recipes are based mainly on traditional French and Italian cooking — but anyone who takes the trouble to follow our methods will have earned a right to the prestige that goes with 'keeping a good table'.

Each volume in the series contains a glossary of the special cooking terms used. In the course of the series we shall cover everything you need to know about meal planning, garnishes, herbs and spices and the preparation of all kinds of food. We haven't neglected drinks and preserving is also included. The basis of good cooking is an international tradition. It is a skill that is fundamental to home-making and to successful entertaining alike.

Glossary of Cooking Terms

Al dente
Italian expression meaning just tender but not soft ('to the tooth'). To test, press the food (usually pasta or rice) with the thumbnail; it should cut cleanly.

Anchovy
Canned anchovies need desalting before use. Soak or wash them very thoroughly in water or milk and dry on absorbent paper. Scrape them to remove all the scales and cut into small fillets or use as required according to the recipe.

Bain-marie
Literally a 'water bath'. Consists of a pan of hot water in which another pan or pans may be stood for cooking. Used for cooking sauces and custards that may curdle if cooked too quickly over direct heat, and for keeping sauces warm without further cooking.

Baste, to
To spoon hot liquid over food as it cooks, to keep it moist and flavoursome.

Bouquet garni
A bundle of herbs, traditionally tied together with string round their stalks, but now more usually wrapped in muslin. The herbs are removed from the dish before it is served. Bouquets garnis of dried herbs are often sold in sachets.

Caramelize, to
To boil sugar to the stage where it turns brown. Caramel is used to colour and flavour many dishes and sauces.

Croûtons
Small pieces of bread or potato, toasted or fried and used as a garnish for a hot meat dish or a soup.

Flame, to
To pour flaming spirit or fortified wine over food. The spirit must first be warmed so that it will ignite, then when alight it is poured over the food. This burns the alcohol out of the liquor but concentrates its flavour.

Foie gras
Livers of force-fed geese, used to make the most choice of pâtés.

Gratiné, to
To brown the top of a dish. The food is generally sprinkled with breadcrumbs, butter and sometimes grated cheese, then placed in a hot oven or under a preheated grill to brown. A fireproof dish with handles at either end is known as a gratin dish.

Julienne strips
Small matchstick shapes of vegetable, meat or other food, usually for use as a garnish.

Knead, to
To work a dough (bread or pastry) with knuckles of one hand. The aim is to break air bubbles formed during rising and to develop the gluten in the dough.

Parboil, to
To cook partly, by boiling, prior to completing cooking by some other method. This is to ensure that the food is soft right to the centre.

Purée
A thick cream made by forcing food through a sieve or working it in a blender.

Reduce, to
To boil a liquid fast, thereby reducing the quantity and concentrating the flavour.

Sauté, to
To brown food quickly in butter or oil and butter. Sometimes cooking is finished in the sauce that is made with the food in the sauté pan.

Tomatoes
To peel tomatoes, first dip them in boiling water for 10–12 seconds to loosen the skin. Alternatively, hold the tomato on a fork in the flame of a gas jet, turning it until the skin is scorched all over; it will then peel easily.

Worcestershire Sauce
Commercially made, bottled sauce based on soy sauce and well spiced. Used in flavouring meat dishes and pies.

Glossary of Vegetables

Vegetables play an extremely important part in our diet. Not only do we need to eat them but the meats and dairy foods we eat come from other animals which feed almost entirely on vegetation; our whole body structure can therefore be said to depend to a large extent on vegetable foodstuffs.

While meat, milk foods and eggs supply us with protein and fats, it is vegetables that supply almost all we need of minerals and vitamins. While it is easy enough to keep alive on protein foods alone, it is virtually impossible to keep healthy, either physically or mentally, without those minerals and vitamins — even those that are required only in trace amounts. On the other hand, even though many people like to eat meat, it is equally possible to keep fit and mentally alert on a totally vegetarian diet.

Cooking Vegetables

It is worth taking extra care when cooking vegetables, for not only is their food value easily destroyed by poor treatment, but they become unappetizing.

Many vegetables are at their best eaten uncooked, when they are crisp and fresh. Those that have to be cooked to make them digestible should never be over-cooked; too much cooking not only renders them unpalatable but almost completely destroys the vitamin and mineral content.

Green vegetables such as cabbage and Brussels sprouts, seed vegetables such as peas and beans, need no more than perhaps half an inch of water in the bottom of the pan and will then cook in the steam created by that and their own moisture. Keeping green vegetables hot after cooking has a detrimental effect on their nutritional value.

Tubers which have to be covered with water to prevent them discolouring, such as potatoes and jerusalem artichokes, should be barely covered and not allowed to cook until they start to break up in the water.

Artichoke

A form of thistle that has been carefully cultivated and improved over hundreds of years until it is now considered a table delicacy. It is the flower part of the artichoke that is eaten, both for its fleshy petals and for the heart or 'fond' of the flower, which is tender and has a very special taste.

Most varieties of artichoke are quite large and a single flower is therefore often served alone as an appetizer; alternatively, the petals may be pulled apart and mixed into a salad or the artichoke hearts may be served as an accompaniment to a meat or fish dish. The whole flower is generally boiled or braised, while the hearts are often sautéed.

Jerusalem Artichoke

Small and irregularly-shaped tuber that has no relation to the true artichoke except a faint similarity in flavour. It is best scrubbed and cooked in its skin, and the skin then rubbed off before serving.

Asparagus

Spear-shaped vegetable with a hard woody stalk, up to 8 or 9 inches long depending on the variety, and a tender tip. In some varieties the stalk is virtually inedible, in others it may be quite tender. For cooking, the spears are tied in bundles and the ends all cut to the same length; the bundle should then be stood upright in a tall pan of boiling salted water, with the spears immersed and the tips above the water. This way it is possible to cook it until the hard stalks are tender, without over-cooking the soft tips.

Asparagus is often served as an appetizer, in which case it is eaten with the fingers and dipped in melted butter or a sauce. It is equally good hot or cold, as an accompanying vegetable or in a salad.

Avocado

Pear-shaped fruit with a large seed, listed here as it is generally used in hors d'oeuvres and salads. The skin is thick, dark green and of a coarse texture unsuitable for eating. The flesh is smooth and almost white but faintly tinged with green.

Serve half an avocado per person, with vinaigrette dressing or stuffed with shrimps, or cut into slices for a salad.

Beans (Fresh and Dried)

Strictly speaking a bean is the kidney-shaped edible seed that comes from an inedible pod. However, there are many vegetables also known as beans in which the pod is edible. The more common varieties are listed below.

French Beans (Haricots Verts) are topped and tailed before cooking and eating whole. The seeds may be extracted and either dried, or canned, as **Kidney** beans **(Flageolets)**.

String, Green or **Snap Beans** Similar to French beans but coarser. Top and tail, slice and remove strings before cooking.

Broad Beans Large and green. The pod is only edible when very young and freshly picked.

Butter Beans and **Small White Haricots** are large seeds from an inedible pod.

Lentil Seed vegetable usually dried for use in wintertime. Dried lentils are usually light orange in colour and a rather flat shape.

Lima Beans These seeds from an inedible pod come fresh or dried. After soaking, the dried ones cook in about the same time as the fresh.

Beans *continued*

Soybeans, Red Kidney Beans and a variety of **White (Haricot) Beans** including **Great Northern, Navy,** and **Pea Beans** are all dried legumes that need soaking according to the package directions before slow simmering.

Bean Sprouts are the newly germinated shoots from bean seeds, usually **Mung,** or **Soya,** beans. The Chinese eat them fresh and they are sometimes obtainable fresh in the West but normally sold canned.

Beetroot

Thick, fleshy root vegetable, generally deep purple in colour. Most commonly eaten as a salad vegetable (cooked and cold) but also hot to accompany hot dishes. Borsch, a beetroot soup, is a national dish of Poland and Russia. Other varieties of beetroot are cultivated for sugar production and cattle food.

Broccoli

Similar to cauliflower, but with a green or purple flower. Some varieties have a large, single flower head like cauliflower; other sprouting varieties carry a number of smaller flower heads on a longer stem. Generally served hot with meat or fish.

Brussels Sprout

Very small, compact cabbage with leaves that curl closely over each other to form a tight ball. The smaller and more freshly picked, the better they taste. Serve hot as an accompaniment to meat dishes.

Cabbage

Vegetable with a large leaf that may be eaten cooked or fresh. The leaves should be separated and washed very thoroughly before use, or if the leaves grow too closely to be separated, shred the whole cabbage finely to wash it. Cabbage should be cooked in a minimum of boiling salted water for the least possible time required to render it just tender, otherwise the entire vitamin content will be destroyed. The most common cabbage varieties are green-leaved, but white and red cabbages are also available. Cabbage is also a good vegetable for pickling.

Cardoon

Type of thistle related to the artichoke. Only the root and ribs of the inner leaves are eaten. If cardoon is not available, celery can be substituted.

Carrot

Long, tapering root vegetable, most commonly orange-coloured. When young, carrots may be eaten fresh as a salad vegetable; as they get older they require cooking to make them digestible. The goodness in a carrot lies almost entirely in and immediately under the skin, which should therefore not be removed for cooking. Instead, scrub the carrots with a hard vegetable brush. If the skin is very unsightly, remove after cooking.

Cauliflower

Variety of cabbage cultivated for its large white flowers. It has very little green leaf, and this is cut almost entirely away before cooking. First soak cauliflower in cold salted water to make sure that any grubs are soaked out, then slit the base of the hard stem, to allow the heat to penetrate more easily, and steam or lightly boil until flower is just tender.

A sauce or melted butter is often served with cauliflower, or it may be lightly cooked and allowed to cool before breaking into flowerets for a salad.

Celeriac (Turnip-rooted Celery)

Variety of celery, the stem base being eaten rather than the stalks. The very tough skin has to be removed but the flesh has a delicate flavour.

Celery

It is the stalks of celery that are eaten and these are 'blanched' by banking up with earth as they grow, or kept in the dark by other means, so that even the fully-grown stalks are white and tender. Young celery is best eaten fresh, when it gets older it needs cooking but is one of the few vegetables that is best not cooked by boiling — but by braising in a well flavoured stock. Celery also makes excellent soup and is a good flavouring ingredient for stews.

Chickpea

The seeds, or peas, of the chickpea are used fresh and dried, mostly in soups and stews.

Chicory

Another plant that is blanched while growing, like celery, so that its leaves are silvery white at the base and yellow at the tips. The flavour is bitter but refreshing and chicory is most commonly eaten fresh as a salad vegetable, although it can be braised for serving as an accompaniment.

Cucumber

Long, thin vegetable with a watery flesh that is pleasantly refreshing when eaten fresh as a salad vegetable. The skin contains a substance that aids digestion, and the vegetable is therefore best prepared by washing and slicing with the skin on, rather than by peeling. There is little food value in cucumber. It may also be cooked for serving with hot dishes.

Eggplant (aubergine)

Elongated, gourd-like vegetable with a deep purple skin. It may be baked, grilled, braised or fried, or stuffed with a spicy meat mixture.

Endive

Crisp, fresh-flavoured salad vegetable the shape of a lettuce. The leaves are small, sharply toothed and curled, and have a more pronounced flavour than lettuce. The heart is sometimes blanched while growing to keep it white and tender.

Fennel
The roots of this plant are treated much as celeriac, the stems as celery. The seeds are used as herbs.

Leek
One of the onion family, but more delicately flavoured than most other varieties. Leeks grow as tall, closely packed leaves and are blanched like chicory while growing so that the lower part remains white and tender. Delicious served with meat dishes or as a flavouring ingredient in soups and stews.

Lentil (see Beans)

Lettuce
The green leaves, which may be round, flat, pointed or curved according to variety, should be broken off – not cut by a steel knife – then washed and dried for salad; they can then be left to 'crisp' in the refrigerator. Lettuce may be cooked.

Lima (see Beans)

Mushroom
Edible fungi of many varieties, both wild and cultivated. Fungi have no real food value but since the flavour of many varieties is excellent, they are widely used to accompany other foods and to flavour sauces. In Britain and the USA we rarely use more than one or two well-known varieties. In Europe they are gathered in the wild and there is much greater knowledge of which types are poisonous and which are not. Very young, fresh mushrooms are good eaten fresh, with a light, oil dressing; larger ones may be grilled, sautéed, baked or used to flavour soups and stews. Large, fleshy mushrooms are good coated in egg and breadcrumbs and fried.

Olive
Mediterranean fruit eaten as a savoury relish as well as in cooked dishes. Oil for culinary use is extracted from the ripe (black) olive.

Onion
No cook can get far without onions in her kitchen. Their properties as flavouring vegetables are unique, blending with almost any meat, fish or other vegetable. Soups and stews are almost invariably flavoured with onion and they may also be used alone, boiled, baked, fried or braised. Fully-grown onion bulbs keep well after pulling and are a staple winter vegetable. The first bulbs are used whole in cooking (button onions) and are favourites for pickling.
Spring onions are used as a salad vegetable.

Pea
Generally, only the seeds of the pea are eaten, though a few varieties have edible pods as well, such as the **Sugar pea (Mange-tout)**. Peas are a favourite vegetable in many parts of the world and respond well to differ-ent methods of preserving, notably freezing. When freshly picked, young garden peas are excellent to eat uncooked, although they tend to be indigestible and are therefore usually cooked and served hot, or cooled for a salad.

Pepper
A hollow vegetable, either round or oblong in shape. All types, whether green, red or yellow, are good as salad ingredients, though they are more digestible if blanched first, and may also be baked and stuffed, fried or included in stews.

Potato
One of the few vegetables that may be served every day – in different ways – without becoming boring. Potatoes contain plenty of food value, though this is mostly in, or next to, the skins. Therefore, unless very old and dirty, potatoes are best cooked in their skins, and peeled after cooking. The skins of new potatoes are pleasant to eat, while the jackets of crisply baked old potatoes are excellent. Potatoes may be served plain boiled, boiled and creamed with butter and milk, steamed, baked, sautéed or fried.

If included in soups and stews no other thickening agent is required. Young, waxy potatoes are good cooked, cooled and dressed with mayonnaise for a salad. Potatoes are one of the world's staple foods.

Pumpkin
Large, fleshy, slightly sweet vegetable good in soups, and as an accompanying vegetable. Pumpkin pie is the traditional American dessert for Thanksgiving Day.

Radish
Small, crisp root vegetable with white flesh and red skin. Radishes are best pulled young and served fresh with salads; they are not so good cooked.

Salsify
Basically a root vegetable though occasionally the young spring leaves are eaten in salads. The roots are long, thin and white and when boiled are delicately flavoured.

Spinach
Green, large-leafed vegetable with a pronounced and distinctive flavour. Spinach leaves contain a high proportion of water and, after thorough washing, need no extra water for cooking. They should not be used unless very fresh as the leaves quickly wilt and become spoiled in flavour and appearance.

Spring onion (see Onion)

Sweet Potato
Tuber similar in appearance to a large potato, but the flesh is tender, sweet and slightly perfumed. It may be boiled and mashed, roasted or fried.

Tomato

A fruit that is normally treated as a vegetable, the tomato is round, fleshy and usually red. A good tomato is at its best eaten fresh as a salad vegetable. Some varieties lose their flavour if cooked; others are good halved and grilled or sautéed, or stuffed with a spicy meat mixture. Peeled tomatoes add flavour to a casserole dish. Use concentrated purée (paste) as a flavouring ingredient for savoury dishes.

Truffle

Fragrant tuber that grows wild and is found only in certain regions. The truffles of the Périgord district of France are said to be the best. Truffles are rarely eaten alone, but are used to flavour and scent other foods. Foie gras, which doesn't smell particularly good alone, is frequently scented with truffles; they are also added to egg and chicken dishes.

Turnip

Root vegetable, larger than the potato and either long and tapering, or round. The flesh is white and slightly sweet. Turnips are excellent in stews and with rich foods such as duck or goose, they are good roasted in the pan round a cut of meat, or they may be boiled and mashed with butter.

Zucchini

Small variety of edible gourd. Zucchini are generally 5–8 inches long and about $1\frac{1}{4}$ inches in diameter. The flesh is creamy white and the skin, which is not removed for cooking, is green. Slice and sauté in butter, or steam them, and flavour with herbs. Zucchini have little flavour of their own and are therefore not particularly good plain boiled. Zucchini may also be stuffed with a spicy meat mixture, as for tomatoes or eggplant.

Cheeses of the World

Cheese is one of the few foodstuffs that still remain intensely regional. Not that cheeses are not widely distributed, both nationally and internationally, but they still retain regional names and characteristics that are often difficult or even impossible to imitate in other parts of the world.

Cheddar is an exception. The 'Cheddaring' process happens to lend itself well to mechanization and good Cheddar-type cheese is produced as far from its English place of origin – Somerset – as New York, Wisconsin and Canada. At the other extreme are cheeses like French Roquefort, made from the milk of sheep grazed on limestone pastures and matured in the limestone caverns of the Roquefort region. No one has yet succeeded in making an imitation of Roquefort anywhere else in the world. The soil on which the sheep graze, the method of cheese production and the local conditions in which it is matured all have a marked effect on the finished food.

Listed below are some of the most important cheeses of the world, with brief descriptions of their characteristics.

British Cheeses

Blue Dorset Hard cheese made from skimmed milk. It is white with a blue vein and has a rather strong flavour.

Caerphilly Crumbly, whole milk cheese that does not mature well. It is white, mild-flavoured and best eaten fresh, not cooked.

Cheddar Hard, yellow, whole milk cheese, smooth-textured and varying in flavour from mild to quite strong. Farmhouse Cheddar is still considered the best and is usually slightly harder than bulk-produced varieties.

Cheshire A hard cheese. Some types are red and mild-flavoured; if these are allowed to ripen until blue veining appears the flavour becomes very rich. A white Cheshire cheese has a moderate flavour.

Derby Hard, close-textured, white cheese. If eaten young it is mild, but develops a stronger flavour with age. Sage Derby has sage leaves added to produce a green cheese.

Double Gloucester Hard, orange-coloured cheese with a rather crumbly texture. The rich flavour is similar to that of mature Cheddar.

Lancashire Fairly hard cheese but crumbly when cut. Its mild flavour strengthens as the cheese matures.

Leicester Hard, orange-red coloured cheese with a mild, slightly sweet flavour.

Stilton Semi-hard cheese made from rich milk with extra cream added. It is white with a blue veining caused by mould inoculated into the cheese (the same strain of mould as that used in Roquefort). Stilton is made in rounds about 12–14 inches across and 9–10 inches deep; the crust is dull and wrinkled but should not be cracked as this allows the cheese to dry out.

A milder, white Stilton is also available. Neither variety is suitable for cooking.

Wensleydale Another double cream cheese (i.e. made from rich milk with extra cream added). It is a mild, flaky cheese, white, and eaten young.

French Cheeses

Brie Soft farmhouse cheese made from whole milk. It is inoculated with a mould to give it its characteristic flavour and slightly reddish crust. The cheese itself is creamy-coloured, soft, mild and rich; it is made in large flat rounds and sold in wedges. It does not keep, nor does it cook particularly well.

Camembert This is also a farmhouse cheese made from cow's milk and inoculated with mould. It is made in smaller, thicker rounds than Brie; it has the same reddish crust, although the taste is stronger and the texture slightly firmer. It should not look chalky inside, or have too strong a smell.

Demi-Sel Soft cream cheese, sold in square, foil-wrapped packs.

Fromage à la Creme Soft, fresh cream cheese.

Petit Suisse (Petit Gervais) Very mild, unsalted cream cheese sold in small, cylindrical packs. Petits Suisses are often used in sweet dishes with fruit, or served plain with sugar.

Pommel Unsalted double cream cheese, not unlike Petit Suisse.

Pont-l'Evêque Soft cheese that is salted repeatedly during maturing. Like Camembert, it should be eaten while it is still soft and not over-ripe. Made in small squares.

Port-Salut Semi-hard round cheese, creamy yellow in colour and with a mild flavour. It should be eaten while still slightly soft.

Roquefort Made from ewe's milk layered with a culture of moulded breadcrumbs. It is made only in the lambing season and only in the Roquefort district. The end result is a whitish, curd-like cheese, mottled with blue veins. The taste is sharp.

Swiss Cheeses

Emmenthal Also made in Italy and Austria, this hard, smooth-textured cheese has large 'eyes' or holes caused by the rapid fermentation of the curd. The colour is a pale yellow, the flavour distinctive. Emmenthal cooks extremely well and is often used in conjunction with Parmesan to give the combination of a creamy texture and sharp flavour to a dish.

Gruyère Also made in the USA and France, where it has large holes resembling Swiss Emmenthal, and in Italy. Although similar to Emmenthal, the 'eyes' are much smaller. The flavour is distinguishable if you have the two side by side, that of Gruyère being sharper.

Italian Cheeses

Bel Paese. Rich, creamy cheese with a mild flavour.

Dolcelatte Very mild, creamier form of Gorgonzola.

Gorgonzola Semi-hard, blue-veined cheese with a sharp flavour.

Mozzarella Semi-soft cheese with a mild flavour that is excellent for cooking.

Parmesan The most famous of Italian cheeses, and the hardest of all. It is a pale straw colour and is full of tiny pin-prick holes. As its flavour is very strong and characteristic, even when grated very finely, it is often used to add flavour to cooked dishes. (**Pecorino** can be substituted for Parmesan.)

Ricotta Soft cheese with a mild flavour not unlike creamed cottage cheese, often used for savoury and sweet fillings.

Dutch Cheeses

Edam Firm, smooth cheese with a mild flavour. The cheeses are made in a ball shape, deep yellow inside, and with a bright red skin on the outside. It cooks quite well.

Gouda This is both creamier and tastier than Edam, though a cut portion of Gouda might look much the same. The whole cheeses are larger and have a yellow skin. Some smaller cheeses are made for export.

Scandinavian Cheeses

Danish Blue White, crumbly cheese with blue veining produced by the introduction of a mould. The flavour is sharp and rather salty.

Havarti (Danish). Smooth, light yellow cheese with lots of large and small holes. Full-flavoured. Sold in a foil package.

Jarlsberg The Scandinavian answer to the high price of Swiss cheeses. Jarlsberg resembles Gruyère and Emmenthal in flavour, though it is slightly milder; the texture is a little softer and there are large and small holes in the cheese.

Mycella (Danish). Mild cheese, pale yellow in colour, with green veining.

Mysöst (Norwegian). Hard, dark brown goats' milk cheese. The flavour is slightly sweet but so strong that it is always eaten in very thin slivers.

Samso (Danish). A firm cheese with even-sized holes. The flavour is mild, sweet and slightly nut-like.

11

Preserving

Most women who regard themselves as homemakers will enjoy preserving. You can serve your chutneys, vinegars and preserves with cold meats, roasts, cheese and savouries. Not only will the flavours be different from the run-of-the-mill commercially made preserves, but they will most likely have a higher nutritional value and cost less.

Herb Vinegars

These are delicious for flavouring salads and for adding to dressings and sauces. Very few varieties are widely available in food stores, but at home you can experiment with all your favourite herbs. The recipes given in our section on herb vinegars use basil, mint, tarragon, rosemary, cloves and bay, along with various spices, but many variations are possible. Use good quality wine vinegars and pick the herbs just before the plants flower for this is when the leaves have the finest flavour. In some cases you can use dried herbs but the results will always be much better with fresh ones.

To make flavoured vinegar you must steep the herbs in vinegar for days or weeks and then strain the mixture before use. While the herbs are being steeped, keep them in the dark. To do this you can either use an opaque jar such as an earthenware one, or dark glass; or you can wrap each jar in paper to exclude the light. A dark cupboard will also do so long as it is not being constantly opened. Once strained, the vinegar is best put into small bottles so that it is handy to use. If the flavour is too strong, you can dilute it with more vinegar before rebottling.

Pickled Vegetables

When pickling vegetables be sure always to select the best quality produce. It is worthless to try to preserve damaged food or that which is past its best; all vegetables should be firm and healthy, clean and dry. If the vegetables have to be washed or wiped, be sure always to dry them thoroughly before starting the preserving process.

For vegetables that have to be soaked in brine, use the best quality rock salt rather than free running table salt. The additives in table salt, which are what keep it fine grained and free running, while not harmful in any way, do not give the best brine for pickling. Rock salt can be bought in crystal form or in blocks, which should be ground by rubbing on a grater or by cutting the block in half and rubbing the two halves together.

Again, the best quality vinegar should be used. Cheap brands may not contain sufficient acetic acid to preserve the vegetables. Wine vinegar has a delicate flavour that will not mask that of the vegetables, but white malt distilled vinegar can also be used quite successfully.

Chutney

Fresh, good quality vegetables, the best vinegar and careful mixing of spices will put you well on the way towards making a good chutney. The remainder of the story is in the cooking. Chutneys need to be cooked until all the ingredients are broken down and well blended and the liquid is evaporated to leave a thick purée. A heavy, wide preserving pan and slow, steady simmering, sometimes for several hours, are what will help you achieve good results. Stir the chutney from time to time as it cooks, to make sure it is not sticking to the bottom of the pan, and cook it slowly and carefully until it is the correct consistency. Like all pickles, it will then need a little time in the jar before it is sufficiently matured to make good eating.

General Rules

Pickling must always be carried out under the right conditions, to keep the food wholesome and safe to eat. Here are the important points to remember.

Vinegar is a highly corrosive liquid and will quickly eat into many metals, forming poisonous substances. Aluminium and stainless steel will resist corrosion from vinegar for the limited period a chutney might be in the pan; our recipes recommend an earthenware or enameled pan, but never use chipped enameled pans as the vinegar will quickly reach the steel or iron beneath. True pickle jar lids are coated with a special vinegar resistant substance, and only this type of screwtop should be used. If not available, use corks for narrow necked bottles or several thicknesses of wax paper tied firmly in place with string, for wide necked jars. Alternatively, you may be able to obtain a special parchment called 'pickling skin' which is slightly less porous than paper, and very useful if you do a lot of preserving.

Any type of jar can be used for chutney and most households have a stock of empty jam jars. However, these are not always suitable for vegetable pickles. For these you need really wide necked jars so that you can put in the whole vegetables or slices without breaking them. Special pickle jars can be bought; these are usually square, which makes storage more convenient.

All jars should be thoroughly washed and sterilized before use with boiling water. Never pour boiling chutney or vinegar into a cold jar as it will crack. Warm the jar first under the hot tap or in a low oven.

Herb and Spice Chart

HERBS AND SPICES	Meat	Fish	Poultry and Game	Soup	Vegetables	Salads and Dressings	Cheese	Eggs	Sauces	Preserves	Cakes and Pies
ALLSPICE	*	*		*	*	*	*	*	*	*	*
BASIL	**	*		**	*	*		*	*		
BAY	**	**	*	***					**		
CAYENNE	*	*	*	*	*				*		
CHERVIL	*	*	*	*	*	**	*	*	*		
CHILLI	*		*						*	*	
CHIVES	*	*	*	*	*	***	*	*	*		
CINNAMON	*							*		*	*
CLOVES	*		*	*	*				*	*	*
DILL	*	**	*	*	*	**	*	*	*	*	
GARLIC	**	*	*	**	*	*			**		
JUNIPER			*		*						
MACE	*	*	*	*	*		*		*	*	*
MARJORAM	*	*	*	*	*	*	*	*	*		
MINT	*		*		*	*			*		
MUSTARD	*			*		*	*	*	*	*	
NUTMEG	*	*	*		*			*	*		
OREGANO	*	**	*	*	**	*	*	*	*		
PAPRIKA	*	*	*	*	*	*	*	*	*		
PARSLEY	**	**	**	***	*	*		*	**		
PEPPER	**	**	**	*	**	**	*	*	**	**	
ROSEMARY	*	*	*	*	*		*				
SAFFRON	*	*	*	*	*	*		*		*	
SAGE	*		*	*			*				
TARRAGON	*	**	*		*				*	*	
THYME	*	*	*		*	*	*	*			
TURMERIC	*	*			*			*	*	*	*

* Indicates type of food with which herb or spice is best used.

Index

Page references to photographs are printed in **heavy** type.

Note: all quantities given are for 4 servings unless otherwise stated.
Approximate metric equivalents to all measures are given in brackets.

Asparagus au Gratin

Ingredients: *4 lb (2 kg) asparagus · salt · pepper · 4 oz (115 g) butter · 1 glass dry white wine · 4 oz (115 g) cooked ham, cut into strips · 2 tablespoons grated Parmesan cheese*

Trim the bottom off each stalk of asparagus to make them all the same length, scrape the white part, wash well and tie the stalks together in small bundles. Cook for 15–20 minutes until tender in plenty of boiling salted water, with the green tops out of the water, and the pan partly covered. Drain and arrange in an ovenproof dish (step 1). Sprinkle with salt and pepper, add ¾ of the melted butter, the wine (step 2), ham and Parmesan (step 3). Dot with remaining butter. Put the asparagus in a hot oven (400°F/gas 6) to gratiné for about 10 minutes.

Asparagus Vinaigrette

Prepare and boil the asparagus as above, place on a serving dish, sprinkle with chopped parsley and serve with a vinaigrette dressing (3 parts oil to 1 part vinegar or lemon juice, salt and pepper to taste).

Asparagus with Eggs

Prepare and boil 4 lb (2 kg) asparagus as above. Leave to dry on a napkin (they can be served either hot or cold) then arrange on a serving dish with the tips toward the centre of the dish. Mash 4 hard-boiled eggs with a fork, and mix them with plenty of vinaigrette dressing. Pour over the tips of the asparagus.

Asparagus with Mousseline Sauce

Prepare and boil 4 lb (2 kg) asparagus as above. Meanwhile, make the mousseline sauce: dilute 3 egg yolks in a little water in a small saucepan, over very low heat. Beat gently with a wire whisk, gradually adding 8 oz (225 g) butter in small pieces, and from time to time 1 teaspoon cold water to make the sauce lighter. When all the butter has been absorbed, remove the sauce from the heat, add 1 tablespoon lemon juice, salt and white pepper to taste, and whip in 3 tablespoons double cream. Drain the asparagus and serve with the mousseline sauce.

Aspic Aurora

Ingredients: *1 tablespoon powdered gelatin ·
1 lb (500 g) tomatoes, chopped · 1 small onion,
chopped · 1 celery stick, chopped · 1 clove ·
1 bouquet garni made of parsley, thyme and
1 bay leaf · ½ teaspoon sugar · salt · pepper ·
juice of ½ lemon · hard-boiled eggs · pitted
black olives · tomatoes · gherkins · carrots,
green peas and cauliflower flowerets, all cooked*

To garnish: *olives · lemon · parsley*

Soak the gelatin in a little cold water in a
heatproof bowl. Meanwhile, put the tomatoes
in a pan with the onion, celery, clove, bouquet
garni, sugar, salt and pepper to taste, and a
little water. Cook very slowly for about ½ hour,
then work through a vegetable mill or sieve,
and add enough water to obtain 1 pint (½ l)
sauce. Return to the heat, bring to the boil and
remove from the heat immediately. Strain the
sauce through a cloth into a measuring jug
and, if there is less than 1 pint (½ l), add a little
hot water. Stand the bowl containing the gelatin in a pan of hot water and allow to dissolve
over low heat. Mix it with the tomato sauce
(step 1), and add the lemon juice. Pour a
¼-inch layer of this tomato aspic into the bottom of a large round mould, and put the mould
in the refrigerator. As soon as it has set, arrange
carefully over the aspic slices of egg, olive,
tomato, gherkin, carrot and a few green peas
and cauliflower flowerets (step 2). Pour over
another thin layer of aspic (step 3), and let it
set in the refrigerator. Repeat these layers
until all the ingredients have been used,
finishing with a layer of aspic. Keep in the
refrigerator until serving time. To unmould:
turn the mould over on a large serving dish,
and cover it with a cloth soaked in boiling
water and squeezed; or, plunge the mould in
hot water for a few seconds. When the aspic
has dropped onto the dish, return to the
refrigerator for a few minutes. Garnish with
whole olive, slices of lemon and parsley sprigs.

Aspic à la Russe

Peel 6 oz (175 g) carrots and 6 oz (175 g)
turnips and cut into strips. Cover with boiling
salted water and cook until tender. Meanwhile,
cover 9 oz (270 g) each of green peas and beans
with boiling salted water, add 1 tomato

together with 1 onion stuck with 1 clove, and
1 bouquet garni, and cook until peas and
beans are tender. Drain vegetables and
reserve both cooking liquids. Put reserved
cooking liquids into a clean pan and continue
boiling, with the bouquet garni and 1 celery
stick until reduced. Soak 1 tablespoon powdered gelatin in cold water. Strain the vegetable

stock through a cloth once it has reduced to
1 pint (½ l). Check the seasoning. Stir the soaked
gelatin into the stock and stir to dissolve. Put a
layer of this vegetable aspic at the bottom of a
large round mould, and let it set in the refrigerator. Proceed as for the above recipe, placing
layers of vegetables and vegetable aspic alter-
nately in the mould. Unmould as above.

1

2

3

Beetroot Salad with Onions

Ingredients: *2 medium-sized beetroots, cooked · 2 medium-sized onions · marjoram · ½ clove of garlic, chopped*

For the vinaigrette dressing: *oil · vinegar · salt · pepper · mustard (optional)*

Peel the beetroots and the onions, cut the beetroots into thin slices and the onions into rings (steps 1 and 2). Toss in a generous amount of vinaigrette dressing (see p.36), and arrange in a salad bowl with the marjoram and garlic (step 3). Alternatively, use cooked onions — bake them, unpeeled, in a moderately hot oven (375°F/gas 5) for 1½ hours then use as raw onion, omitting marjoram and garlic.

Sour Beetroots

Peel and cut into very thin slices 2 medium-sized cooked beetroots. Put in a flameproof dish, and sprinkle with salt and pepper. Add ½ pint (¼ l) sour cream, or double cream seasoned a few hours before with lemon juice. Put the dish in a hot oven (400°F/gas 6), until the cream begins to boil and thicken. Serve immediately.

Sweet-and-Sour Beetroots

Peel and dice 2 medium-sized cooked beetroots. Sauté lightly in melted butter. Add 1 teaspoon sugar and 2 tablespoons vinegar. Continue cooking for a few minutes. Serve immediately.

Beetroots à l'Anglaise

Blanch 4 small cooked beetroots in boiling water for a few minutes. Drain and peel. Cut into thick slices and serve with fresh butter.

Stuffed Beetroots

Peel and halve lengthwise 4 or more small cooked beetroots, and remove part of the flesh in the centre. Fill with Russian, chicken or fish salad mixed with mayonnaise (commercially prepared or home-made). Arrange the beetroots on a serving dish and garnish with lettuce leaves tossed in vinaigrette dressing. Keep in a refrigerator or cool place before serving.

Glazed Beetroots

Peel and dice (or cut into balls with a melon ball cutter) 2 medium-sized cooked beetroots. Sauté for 3–4 minutes in melted butter. Sprinkle with 1 tablespoon sugar, and continue to cook for a few more minutes, shaking the pan from time to time to ensure that beetroots are evenly glazed. Serve immediately.

Beetroots au Gratin

Peel and slice 2 medium-sized cooked beetroots. Put in a buttered ovenproof dish alternating layers of beetroots, béchamel sauce (see p.33) and grated Parmesan cheese. Finish with a layer of béchamel and Parmesan, and dot with butter. Put in moderate oven (350°F/gas 4) for 15–20 minutes, or until golden.

1

2

3

Broccoli Niçoise

Ingredients: *3 lb (1½ kg) broccoli · oil ·*
1 onion, thinly sliced · 4 oz (115 g) black
olives, pitted and sliced · 8 anchovy fillets,
desalted by soaking in a little milk · 3 oz (90 g)
Gruyère cheese, grated · salt · pepper ·
½ pint (¼ l) good red wine preferably Burgundy

Wash the broccoli and cut into flowerets (step
1). Put ¼ of the broccoli in a flameproof
casserole (preferably earthenware) with 1
tablespoon oil, ½ the onion, a few slices of
olive, and a few pieces of anchovy. Add
another layer of broccoli to the casserole
and sprinkle generously with ½ the grated
cheese (step 2). Add another tablespoon oil
and salt and pepper to taste. Repeat layers
once more, then pour over the wine (step 3).
Cover, and cook very slowly on top of the stove
or in a moderate oven (350°F/gas 4) for 1 hour,
or until the broccoli is tender and has absorbed
most of the cooking juices. Serve in the cooking
dish.

Golden Broccoli

Wash 2 lb (1 kg) broccoli and cut into flowerets.
Cover with boiling salted water and cook gently
until *al dente.* Drain, rinse in cold water, put on a
paper napkin to dry, then roll in flour, and
dip in egg beaten with a little salt and pepper.
Fry a few at a time in very hot deep oil until
golden. Lift out of the oil with a slotted spoon,
drain on a paper napkin, and serve on a warm
serving dish garnished with parsley and
lemon quarters.

Broccoli Pudding

Wash 3 lb (1½ kg) broccoli and cut into flowerets. Peel and slice 1 lb (500 g) potatoes and 1
large onion. Peel 1 lb (500 g) tomatoes and
chop roughly. Put a few tablespoons olive oil
in the bottom of a flameproof dish (preferably
earthenware) and add onion, potatoes, broccoli
and tomatoes in layers, ending with a layer of
tomatoes. Spoon oil over top of vegetables,
sprinkle with salt and pepper. Add 1 glass
water, cover, and cook slowly on top of stove
or in a moderate oven (350°F/gas 4) for about
1 hour, or until vegetables are tender. Shake
the dish from time to time during cooking.
Serve immediately in the cooking dish.

Glazed Turnips

Wash 1½ lb (750 g) young white turnips and
pare in the shape of large olives. Brown in butter, adding a pinch of salt and 1 teaspoon sugar.
Add beef stock to cover half the turnips,
cover the pan and continue cooking on very
low heat until all the juice has evaporated.
Add more butter to taste and serve.

Turnips with Garlic and Cheese

Peel and wash thoroughly 4 lb (2 kg) turnips.
Sauté lightly in a frying pan 2 cloves of garlic,
crushed, in oil. Add the turnips, salt and
pepper to taste, cover and cook slowly for
about ¾ hour, adding a few tablespoons water
if turnips become dry. Sprinkle with grated
Parmesan cheese before serving.

1

2

3

Stuffed Artichokes

Ingredients: *8 medium-sized artichokes · juice of 1 lemon · $\frac{1}{2}$ pint ($\frac{1}{4}$ l) stock · 2 tablespoons oil*

For the stuffing: *4 oz (115 g) tongue or cooked ham, diced · 4 oz (115 g) mozzarella or Gruyère cheese, diced · 4 tablespoons fresh white breadcrumbs, fried in butter · 4 tablespoons grated Parmesan cheese · 1 egg yolk · chopped parsley · salt · pepper · oil*

To garnish: *sprigs of watercress (optional)*

Remove the stems of the artichokes and the outer leaves, and cut off the tips of the remaining leaves. Put in water mixed with the lemon juice (step 1). Prepare the stuffing: mix the diced meat and cheese in a bowl with the breadcrumbs, Parmesan, egg yolk, and parsley, salt and pepper to taste, and enough oil to obtain a smooth paste. Drain the artichokes well, and either remove the chokes, or spread the leaves out carefully with the fingers. Put the prepared stuffing into the centres of the artichokes piling it up in the middle (step 2). Press back into shape around the stuffing. Put the artichokes in an ovenproof casserole (step 3). Add the stock and the oil, cover, and cook slowly in a moderate oven (350°F/gas 4) for about 1 hour, basting from time to time with the cooking juices. To gratiné the artichokes, uncover the casserole for the last few minutes of cooking. Serve on a warm serving dish, garnished with watercress, if liked.

Artichokes Argenteuil

Prepare and soak 8 medium-sized artichokes as for Stuffed Artichokes. Boil them in salted water for 25 minutes, then drain, cool and remove all the leaves and the choke from the centre. Prepare and cook 1 lb (500 g) asparagus (see p.17), and drain well. Meanwhile, prepare a béchamel sauce (see p.33) and add 2 tablespoons grated Gruyère cheese. Check for seasoning and add salt and pepper if necessary. Fill the artichoke hearts with the asparagus tips. Cover with the béchamel sauce and sprinkle with 1 tablespoon grated Gruyère cheese. Gratiné in a hot oven 400°F/gas 6) for a few minutes and serve immediately in the cooking dish.

Artichokes alla Giudea

Prepare 8 medium-sized artichokes as above, and put them in water mixed with the juice of 1 lemon. Drain well, and spread out the leaves with the fingers. Sprinkle with salt and pepper. Put about $2\frac{1}{2}$ inches oil in a flameproof earthenware casserole or deep frying pan. Heat the oil – but do not let it smoke – and put in the artichokes upside down (the oil should come halfway up the artichokes). Cook on moderate heat, turning them over once after a few minutes, then turning more frequently for about 20 minutes. Return artichokes to original position, squeeze them delicately, and continue cooking on higher heat until they are well browned and crisp. Drain, and serve piping hot with lemon quarters.

1

2

3

Artichokes Clamart

Ingredients: *8 medium-sized artichokes · juice of 1½ lemons · 2 tablespoons flour · 1 teaspoon salt · 3 oz (90 g) butter or margarine · 8 tablespoons fresh or frozen green peas · 4 tablespoons tomato paste, or canned tomatoes, sieved · 2 oz (60 g) cooked ham, diced · 4 oz (115 g) mozzarella cheese, diced*

Prepare the artichokes as for Stuffed Artichokes (see p.21) and put in water mixed with the juice of 1 lemon. Drain well and either remove the choke or spread the leaves out carefully with the fingers. Mix the flour with a little cold water, add 1 quart (1 l) cold water, pass through a fine sieve into a pan, add the remaining lemon juice, the salt, 1½ oz (45 g) butter or margarine and the prepared artichokes and cook until artichokes are *al dente* (at least 25 minutes). Drain well, sauté lightly in ¼ of the butter or margarine (step 1), remove from heat and keep warm. Put the peas in a pan of boiling salted water, and cook gently until tender. Drain well, then sauté in remaining butter or margarine. Add the tomato paste or canned tomatoes, and continue cooking for 5 minutes. Add the ham and continue cooking for a further 5 minutes to reduce the sauce. Remove from the heat, add the mozzarella cheese (step 2), and spread the mixture in and around the artichoke hearts (step 3). Cover, and keep on low heat for a few minutes.

Artichokes Barigoule

Prepare and soak 8 medium-sized artichokes as above, and cook for 10 minutes in 2 inches of boiling salted water. Drain well. Remove the choke from the centre. Chop finely 4 oz /115 g) onion, 4 oz (115 g) carrots, 6 oz (175 g) mushrooms, 6 oz (175 g) lean salt pork (previously soaked in cold water for 1 hour), and cook gently in 3 oz (90 g) butter. Add 2 tablespoons tomato paste and 2 crushed cloves of garlic. Continue cooking for a few more minutes, and season to taste. Fill the artichokes with the mixture, wrap them in thin slices of pork fat, tie them with string, and put them in an ovenproof dish. Pour over ½ pint (¼ l) dry white wine, and cook in a moderate oven (350°F/ gas 4) for 1 hour, basting often. Remove strings and pork fat, arrange artichokes on a dish and pour over the cooking juices.

1

2

3

1   2   3

Tomato Pie

Ingredients: for the pastry, *6 oz (175 g) flour · salt · 3 oz (90 g) butter or margarine · 3 tablespoons cold water*

For the filling: *1 lb (500 g) tomatoes, preferably Italian plum type · 1 onion, chopped · 1 clove of garlic, crushed · 1 bouquet garni made of parsley, basil and 1 bay leaf · salt · pepper*

For the mornay sauce: *1 oz (30 g) butter or margarine · 1 tablespoon flour · 1 glass milk · salt · pepper · 2 oz (60 g) grated Gruyère cheese*

To garnish: *sprig of basil or parsley (optional)*

Prepare the dough: sift the flour with a pinch of salt onto a working surface or pastry board. Add the butter or margarine, cut into pieces, and work into the flour with the fingers until the mixture resembles fine breadcrumbs. Add the water gradually until a firm dough is formed, knead and roll dough into a ball, wrap in wax paper and let stand in a cool place or refrigerator for ½ hour. Meanwhile, dip the tomatoes in boiling water, peel them, seed them, and cut them into pieces (step 1). Put in a pan together with the onion, garlic, bouquet garni, and salt and pepper to taste. Cook uncovered for ¾ hour or until mixture becomes a thickish purée. Meanwhile, flatten out the dough with a rolling pin to a thickness of ¼ inch and use to line the bottom and sides of a cake tin (about 10-inch diameter). Prick the bottom of the dough with a fork, cover with wax paper or aluminium foil, and put dry beans or rice over the paper so that the dough will not swell. Bake 'blind' in a hot oven (425°F/gas 7) for 25–30 minutes. Meanwhile, prepare mornay sauce: melt the butter or margarine on moderate heat, stir in the flour, cook for 1–2 minutes, remove from the heat and add the cold milk gradually, stirring constantly. Return to heat and cook for 10 minutes, stirring occasionally. Remove from the heat, add salt and pepper to taste, and the cheese. When the pastry is cooked, remove the paper and beans, spread the tomato purée over (step 2), and pipe the mornay sauce over the tomato in an attractive pattern (step 3). (Alternatively the mornay sauce can simply be spooned over.) Put the pie back into the hot oven for 5–8 minutes, or until golden. Serve hot, garnished with a sprig of basil or parsley if liked.

1   2   3

Celery au Gratin

Ingredients: *1 large head of celery · 1 lemon · 2 tablespoons flour · 1 quart (1 l) cold water · salt · 2½ oz (75 g) butter or margarine · Parmesan cheese · 2 glasses milk, or 1 glass milk and 1 glass single cream · pepper*

Remove the coarse ribs of the celery, split and cut stalks into 2-inch pieces. Remove the tough part of the core and slice it. Rub with ½ the lemon (step 1). Cook the celery pieces in the flour, water, juice of remaining ½ lemon, 1 teaspoon salt and ½ the butter or margarine (step 2), on a very low heat for about 1–1½ hours, stirring often. Drain well, arrange in layers in a buttered ovenproof dish, alternating with grated Parmesan cheese (step 3). Add the milk, or milk and cream, sprinkle with grated Parmesan, and salt and pepper to taste and dot with remaining butter or margarine. Put in a moderate oven (350°F/gas 4) for ½ hour, or

until golden and cooking liquid has evaporated. Serve hot in the cooking dish.

Celery Bolognese

Prepare 1 head of celery as above, and cook it in the water and flour mixture until tender. Meanwhile, prepare a Bolognese or tomato sauce (see p.41). Drain celery, dry well, and dip in egg beaten with a little salt, then in flour. Fry in very hot deep oil. Arrange in a buttered ovenproof dish layers of celery, Bolognese sauce, grated Parmesan cheese and pieces of butter, ending with a layer of cheese and butter. Put in a hot oven (425°F/gas 7) for 20–25 minutes, or until a golden crust forms on the surface.

Celery Fritters

Prepare a batter: mix 1 whole egg and 2 egg yolks with 6 oz (175 g) flour, ½ pint (¼ l) beer and 1 tablespoon oil. Season with salt and pepper, and let stand for 2 hours. Meanwhile, prepare 1 large head of celery and put in water mixed with lemon juice. Cook for about 1½ hours in boiling salted water. Add 2 egg whites whisked until stiff to the batter and chopped parsley to taste. Dip the celery sticks into the batter and fry them in deep hot oil until golden. Drain on absorbent paper.

Celery with Hollandaise Sauce

Prepare and cook 2 lb (1 kg) celery until tender, as above; drain well. Arrange on a dish, and serve with Hollandaise sauce.

Creamed Carrots

Ingredients: *2 lb (1 kg) carrots · ½ pint (¼ l) hot water · salt · 2 oz (60 g) butter or margarine · 2 egg yolks · 4 fl oz (100 ml) single cream · 1 tablespoon chopped parsley*

To garnish: *sprigs of parsley*

Scrape and wash the carrots; leave them whole if they are young and small, or slice them if they are large. Place in a pan, add the hot water (step 1), a pinch of salt, and ½ the butter or margarine (step 2), and cook, covered, for about ½ hour, or until tender. Stir from time to time, and take care that the cooking liquid is not completely absorbed. When the carrots are tender, remove from the heat, add the egg yolks mixed with the cream, remaining butter or margarine (melted) and the chopped parsley (step 3). Return to heat and continue cooking very gently until the cream has thickened – do not let it boil. Serve immediately garnished with sprigs of parsley.

Carrots Vichy

Prepare 2 lb (1 kg) carrots as above. Put in a pan with 1 quart (1 l) water, 3 oz (60 g) butter or margarine, a pinch of salt and 3 lumps sugar. Boil, uncovered, until all the water has evaporated and the butter begins to fry. Sprinkle with chopped parsley and serve.

Sautéed Carrots

Prepare 2 lb (1 kg) carrots as above, and put in cold salted water to cover. Bring to the boil and continue cooking for about ½ hour or until tender. Drain, leave to cool slightly, then cut into thin slices. Sauté in 2 oz (60 g) butter or margarine. Season with salt to taste, sprinkle with vinegar, boil to evaporate, and serve.

Glazed Carrots

Prepare 2 lb (1 kg) carrots as above. Put in a pan, cover with cold water, cover the pan, and cook until they are tender, or the water is absorbed. Add 1 pinch salt, 2 oz (60 g) butter or margarine, 2 tablespoons honey or sugar, and continue cooking, uncovered, stirring from time to time, until the carrots are golden. (If liked, sprinkle with 1 teaspoon vinegar.)

Purée Crécy

Scrape and wash 1½ lb (750 g) carrots. Put in cold water and bring to the boil. After 15 minutes, add ½ lb (225 g) potatoes, peeled. When carrots and potatoes are tender, drain, and pass through a fine sieve. Add 4 oz (115 g) butter or margarine and 4 fl oz (100 ml) single cream. Mix well and check the seasoning.

Cauliflower Gourmet

Ingredients: *1 medium-sized cauliflower · salt · 1 slice lemon · 1 slice bread · 6 eggs · 5 slices Emmenthal cheese · grated Parmesan cheese · 4 oz (115 g) butter or margarine*

Remove the large outer leaves of the cauliflower and trim the stalk (step 1). Wash thoroughly. Cook in boiling salted water, together with the lemon and bread (to eliminate the cooking smell) until *al dente* (about 15 minutes) and drain. Meanwhile, prepare 3 frittatas (flat, Italian-style omelets, cooked on both sides), each using 2 eggs and about 6 inches in diameter, according to the size of the cauliflower. Arrange the 3 frittatas on an ovenproof serving dish one on top of the other, with 2½ slices of Emmenthal between the first and second frittata and between the second and third (step 2). Place the cauliflower on top, sprinkle with grated Parmesan, pour the butter or margarine over, melted (step 3), and put in a hot oven (425°F/gas 7) for about 10 minutes to gratiné.

Cauliflower au Gratin

Remove the hard outer leaves of a medium-sized cauliflower, keeping the more tender ones, trim the stalk and wash thoroughly. Cook until *al dente* as above. Drain, leave until lukewarm, then divide into flowerets and leave to dry on a clean napkin. Prepare a béchamel sauce (see p.33). Add 1 tablespoon grated Parmesan cheese. Arrange the cauliflower flowerets in a buttered ovenproof dish, pour the béchamel sauce over, sprinkle with a mixture of equal quantities of grated Parmesan cheese and breadcrumbs, pour over melted butter and gratiné as above.

Paupiettes of Cauliflower and Ham

Prepare and cook 1 medium-sized cauliflower as above. Drain, leave until lukewarm then divide into flowerets, and leave to dry on a clean napkin. Wrap each floweret in a small slice of cooked ham or prosciutto, securing with a toothpick or skewer if necessary. Dip in beaten egg and roll in breadcrumbs. Let stand in a refrigerator or cool place for ½ hour, then brown and cook in golden butter or hot

oil. Drain well (remove toothpick or skewer if used) and serve piping hot. You can also deep fry the flowerets, after dipping them in batter (see Celery Fritters p.24).

Cauliflower with Piquant Sauce

Prepare and cook 1 medium-sized cauliflower as above. Meanwhile, prepare the piquant

sauce: brown 4 oz (115 g) butter lightly in a small pan, remove from the heat, blend in 8 anchovy fillets, desalted by soaking in cold milk, and mashed, return to heat, add ½ tablespoon chopped parsley and mix well. When the cauliflower is *al dente*, drain and arrange on a warm serving dish, pour the sauce over, sprinkle with the juice of ½ lemon, and serve immediately.

Brussels Sprouts with Bacon

Ingredients: *2 lb (1 kg) fresh or frozen Brussels sprouts · juice of ½ lemon · 4 slices smoked bacon, rind and bones removed · 1½ oz (45 g) butter or margarine · salt · pepper · 1 teaspoon chopped parsley*

Prepare the Brussels sprouts for cooking, putting them at once in cold water mixed with the lemon juice. Cook them in plenty of boiling salted water for about 20 minutes until they are *al dente*. Drain (step 1). Cut the bacon into strips (step 2). Brown the butter or margarine in a frying pan, add the bacon and, when it is crisp, add the sprouts (step 3). Season with salt and pepper to taste, and cook slowly until sprouts are heated through and coated in the cooking fat. Transfer to a warm serving dish, sprinkle with chopped parsley and serve immediately.

Brussels Sprouts with Chestnuts

Peel 1 lb (500 g) chestnuts, put in cold salted water with 1 bay leaf, bring to the boil and cook for about ¾ hour. Meanwhile, prepare and cook 2 lb (1 kg) fresh or frozen Brussels sprouts as above. In a pan melt 3 oz (90 g) butter or margarine, add the chestnuts and sprouts, well drained; cook and serve as above.

Sautéed Brussels Sprouts

Prepare for cooking 2 lb (1 kg) fresh or frozen Brussels sprouts as above. Cook in plenty of boiling salted water, with 1 onion, sliced, 1 bay leaf and 2 cloves for about 20 minutes until they are *al dente*. Drain the sprouts (discarding onion, bay leaf and cloves), brown them lightly in 2 oz (60 g) butter or margarine, and serve immediately.

Fried Brussels Sprouts

Prepare for cooking 1½ lb (1 kg) fresh or frozen Brussels sprouts as above. Cook in plenty of boiling salted water for 10 minutes. Drain, roll in flour, then in egg beaten with salt, and then in breadcrumbs. Fry in hot deep oil until golden, lift them out with a slotted spoon, and drain them. Serve with lemon wedges.

Creamed Brussels Sprouts

Prepare and cook 2 lb (1 kg) fresh or frozen Brussels sprouts as above. Drain and sauté lightly in 2 oz (60 g) butter or margarine. Add ½ pint (¼ l) single cream, 2–3 tablespoons grated Parmesan cheese, salt and grated nutmeg to taste. Cook on moderate heat, stirring constantly until the sauce has thickened.

1   2   3

Stuffed Cabbage

Ingredients: 1 large green cabbage · 4 quarts (4 l) boiling water · 2 oz (60 g) butter · 1 tablespoon olive oil · 2 carrots, peeled and thinly sliced · 2 onions, peeled and thinly sliced · 1 bay leaf · 2 fl oz (50 ml) hot stock

For the stuffing: ½ onion, chopped · 2 tablespoons chopped parsley · 2 oz (60 g) butter or margarine · 1 lb (500 g) minced beef or veal · 4 oz (115 g) minced pork loin · 4 oz (115 g) rice · 1 egg, beaten · 1 teaspoon Worcestershire sauce (optional) · salt · pepper · 1 pinch mixed herbs · 8 tablespoons hot stock

Discard the outer leaves of the cabbage, and wash the cabbage under cold running water. Put in a large pan, add the boiling water, let stand for 5 minutes, then drain. Prepare the stuffing: brown the onion and parsley lightly in the butter or margarine. Put the mixture in a bowl, add the meat, rice, egg, Worcestershire sauce (if using), salt and pepper, herbs and the hot stock. Mix well. Trim the bottom part of the cabbage so that it will stand upright. On a wooden board arrange crosswise 2 lengths of string, stand the cabbage upright over the string and spread out the leaves (step 1). Insert the prepared stuffing between the leaves (step 2). Close the leaves, and tie the cabbage with the string (step 3). In a large casserole, melt the butter with the oil, and arrange the carrots and onions in the bottom. Stand the cabbage in the casserole, add the stock and the bay leaf, cover, and cook over moderate heat for about 2 hours until cabbage is tender and cooked through, adding more stock if necessary. When cooked, place the cabbage on a warm serving dish, remove the string, and garnish with the carrots and onions. Serves 6.

Braised Cabbage

Slice 1½ lb (750 g) carrots and ½ lb (225 g) onions. Crush 3 cloves of garlic. Peel and seed 1 tomato. Cut into strips 6 oz (175 g) fresh pork rind. Melt in a large, heavy pan 2 oz (60 g) lard, add the carrots, onions, garlic, tomato and pork rind. Brown quickly. Meanwhile, blanch 1 medium-sized white cabbage, by plunging into boiling salted water for 1 minutes then draining and refreshing under cold running water. (If green cabbage is used, blanching is not necessary.) Put the cabbage in the pan with ½ pint (¼ l) dry white wine and 1 bouquet garni. Season with salt and pepper to taste, add a little water, and bring to the boil. Cover the pan and put in a low oven (300°F/gas 2) for about 2 hours until the cabbage is tender.

Spanish Chickpeas

Ingredients: *1 lb (500 g) chickpeas ·
½ tablespoon sodium bicarbonate · salt · pepper ·
1 slice bread · 2 tablespoons oil · 1 oz (30 g)
butter or margarine · 1 medium-sized onion,
chopped · 6 oz (175 g) canned peeled tomatoes,
chopped · 1 clove of garlic · 1 hard-boiled egg
pepper*

Let the chickpeas stand in plenty of cold water
(step 1) for 24 hours. Drain, sprinkle with
sodium bicarbonate, mix well and leave for
15 minutes. Rinse under cold running water.
Put in a casserole, add 2 quarts (2 l) cold water,
bring to the boil and cook on moderate heat
for about 2 hours until tender, seasoning with
salt to taste towards the end of the cooking.
In another casserole, fry the bread until crisp
in the oil and butter, remove and reserve. Add
the onion, cook until golden, then add the
tomatoes. After a few minutes, add the drained
chickpeas and a few tablespoons of their
cooking liquid. In a mortar crush the clove of
garlic with the fried bread and the yolk of the
hard-boiled egg (step 2). Add 1–2 tablespoons
water to make a smooth mixture, then add to
the chickpeas, together with the chopped
white of the egg (step 3). Cover, and cook for
½ hour, seasoning with salt and pepper.

Chickpea Salad

Prepare 1 lb (500 g) chickpeas for cooking as
above. Put in a pan with 1½ quarts (1½ l) cold
water, bring to the boil, and cook on moderate
heat for about 2 hours until tender. In a bowl
put 1 clove of garlic, crushed, 1 onion,
chopped, 1 tomato and 1 green pepper,
chopped. Add the drained chickpeas. Season
with oil, vinegar, salt, pepper, and mix.

Chickpeas with Pork

Prepare 1 lb (500 g) chickpeas for cooking as
above. In a large pan brown 2 oz (60 g) butter
or margarine with 2 oz (60 g) salt pork, previously soaked in cold water and chopped, and
1 onion, chopped. Add 2 quarts (2 l) cold water
and the chickpeas. Bring to the boil, add 1
quart (1 l) stock, 1 carrot, peeled and chopped,
2–3 celery sticks, cut into strips, 3 sage leaves
and 3 lb (1½ kg) assorted pork meat (spare ribs,
rind, pig's trotter or ear). Season to taste, and
cook over moderate heat for about 2 hours

or until chickpeas and pork are tender. Serve
the chickpeas with the meat and the broth.

Chickpea Purée

Prepare and cook 1 lb (500 g) chickpeas as
above. Peel ½ lb (225 g) potatoes and cook in
boiling water. Drain the chickpeas (reserving
a little of the cooking liquid) and potatoes and

work through a sieve. In a mortar, crush 2
cloves of garlic with 2 egg yolks, and blend in
½ pint (¼ l) olive oil. Add, a little at a time, to the
chickpea and potato purée, beating constantly
until a smooth mixture is obtained, and adding
from time to time a spoonful of the reserved
juices. Add salt and pepper to taste. Sprinkle
with chopped chervil, basil onion, garlic,
parsley and capers. Serve with toast.

2

3

Stuffed Onions

Ingredients: *4 large onions · 1 celery stick, finely chopped · 1 clove of garlic, crushed · 2 sage leaves, finely chopped · 4 tablespoons breadcrumbs · 4 tablespoons grated Parmesan cheese · 1 tablespoon chopped parsley · salt · pepper · 2 oz (60 g) butter or margarine*

Peel the onions and parboil them. Drain, cut the tops off, and scoop out the centres, leaving about ½ inch around the sides (step 1). Chop the scooped-out onion finely (step 2), and sauté lightly over low heat for 6–7 minutes with the celery, garlic and sage. Add the breadcrumbs, continue cooking for 2 minutes, remove from the heat, and mix in the grated Parmesan cheese, parsley, and salt and pepper to taste. Melt ½ the butter or margarine with a little salt and pepper in an ovenproof dish, put in the onions, and fill with the stuffing (step 3). Dot each onion with the remaining butter. Cook in a hot oven (425°F/gas 7) for 30–35 minutes until tender, basting from time to time with the cooking juices. Garnish with sprigs of parsley and tomato wedges before serving. (If liked, chopped leftover meat or sausage meat can be used in the stuffing.) Stuffed onions can be served cold as well as hot, in which case they should be cooked in oil rather than butter.

Glazed Spring Onions

To garnish meat dishes: peel carefully about 30 small spring onions. Put them in a pan, cover with salted water, add 1 oz (30 g) butter and 1 teaspoon sugar. Cook slowly, uncovered. When all the water has been absorbed, the onions are cooked. Continue cooking until caramelized, shaking the pan from time to time.

Fried Onions

To garnish meat dishes: peel and slice onions, separate into rings and dip in flour seasoned with salt. Deep fry in very hot oil (380°F).

Purée Soubise

Peel 1 lb (500 g) onions. Cover with salted water, and cook together with 4 oz (115 g) rice. When both onions and rice are cooked, drain, and work through a fine sieve. Season with salt and pepper to taste. Add 4 oz (115 g) butter and 4 fl oz (100 ml) double cream. Mix well. Serve with croûtons fried in butter.

Haricots with Ham

Ingredients: ¾ lb (350 g) dried haricot beans · 1 ham bone · salt · 4 oz (115 g) pork rind · ½ clove of garlic, crushed · a little onion and parsley, chopped together · 1½ tablespoons oil · 8 oz (225 g) canned tomatoes, sieved · pepper

Soak the beans in cold water overnight. Drain, put in plenty of cold water together with the ham bone and salt, cover, bring to the boil and cook about 1 hour, until beans are tender. Meanwhile, scorch the pork rind, scald in boiling water, cut into pieces, put in a pan, cover with cold water, and cook very slowly until tender. When both the beans and the pork rind are cooked, in a large pan brown the garlic, onion and parsley in the oil. Add the tomatoes (step 1), and season with salt and pepper to taste. Cook for 15 minutes. Drain the beans (reserving the cooking juices) and the pork rind, and add to the tomato mixture with the meat from the ham bone, cut into strips (step 2). Continue cooking over low heat for another 20 minutes, adding a few spoonfuls of the reserved cooking juices from the beans if the mixture becomes too thick (step 3).

Haricots Bretonne

Cook 1 lb (500 g) fresh haricots in lightly salted boiling water until tender, together with 1 onion stuck with 2 cloves. Meanwhile, in a pan, cook 8 shallots, finely chopped, in 4 oz (115 g) butter until transparent, add 4 tomatoes, peeled and crushed, and salt and pepper to taste. When the beans are cooked, drain (discarding onion) and add to tomato mixture. Sprinkle with chopped parsley before serving.

Boston Baked Beans

In a high and narrow earthenware pot, soak 1 lb (500 g) dried kidney beans in cold water overnight. Drain, and cover again with cold water. Cover the pot, put it over moderate heat, and cook slowly for 1 hour. Drain, reserving the water. Put 6 oz (175 g) salt pork in the piece (previously soaked in cold water) at the bottom of the pot, add the beans, add 10 oz (300 g) salt pork (soaked and chopped) and push it into the beans. Mix 4 oz (115 g) molasses with an equal amount of the reserved cooking water, 4 oz (115 g) mustard powder, 1 pinch paprika, and 1 teaspoon chopped onion. Pour into the pot. Cover, and cook for 6 hours in a slow oven (250°F/gas ½). Every hour add a little more of the reserved cooking water from the beans, and stir lightly with a wooden spoon. Remove the cover from the pot for the last hour of cooking so that a golden crust forms on top.

String Beans
with Tomato Sauce

Ingredients: 2 lb (1 kg) string beans · 1 lb (500 g) tomatoes, preferably Italian plum type · 1 slice onion, chopped · 2 cloves of garlic · 2 sage leaves · 2 oz (60 g) butter or margarine · salt · pepper · stock

To garnish: *fresh sage leaves (optional)*

Remove strings and tips of the beans, and wash in cold water. Cook, uncovered, in boiling salted water until tender (step 1); drain. Dip the tomatoes in boiling water, skin, seed and chop them. Brown the onion, garlic and sage leaves lightly in the butter or margarine (step 2). Remove them and discard. Add the string beans, sauté lightly, then add the tomatoes (step 3). Season with salt and pepper to taste, and continue cooking slowly for about 30 minutes, adding hot stock from time to time if necessary. Serve immediately, garnishing serving dish with fresh sage leaves, if liked.

String Beans Lyonnaise

Prepare and cook 2 lb (1 kg) string beans until tender, as above; drain. In a pan, brown 2 oz (60 g) butter or margarine and $\frac{1}{2}$ lb (225 g) onions, thinly sliced. Add the drained string beans, season with salt to taste and heat through.

String Beans with Poulette Sauce

Prepare and cook 2 lb (1 kg) string beans until tender, as above; drain. Melt in a pan 3 oz (90 g) butter or margarine, stir in 1 tablespoon flour, cook for 1–2 minutes, remove from the heat and stir in $\frac{1}{2}$ pint ($\frac{1}{4}$ l) boiling milk, 2 egg yolks, and salt and pepper and chopped parsley to taste. Return to the heat, add the beans, mix well, cook until sauce is thick and beans are heated through and well coated.

Spanish String Beans

Prepare 2 lb (1 kg) string beans for cooking as above. In a pan, brown 2 oz (60 g) butter or margarine with 1 onion, 1 green pepper and 1 garlic clove, all chopped. Add 6 oz (175 g) canned peeled tomatoes worked through a sieve, or a few tablespoons tomato paste

diluted in water. Continue cooking for a few minutes, then add the string beans, 6 oz (175 g) prosciutto or cooked ham cut into strips or diced, and salt and pepper to taste. Cover, and cook slowly until beans are tender, adding stock from time to time if necessary. Transfer to a warm serving dish and garnish the edges of the dish with hard-boiled egg wedges decorated with tiny strips of black olive.

String Beans with Almonds

Prepare and cook 2 lb (1 kg) string beans until tender, as above. Meanwhile, roast 2 oz (60 g) almonds, peeled, in the oven. When the beans are cooked, melt 3 oz (90 g) butter or margarine in a pan, add the drained beans, the almonds, and salt and pepper to taste. Sauté over high heat. Sprinkle with lemon juice.

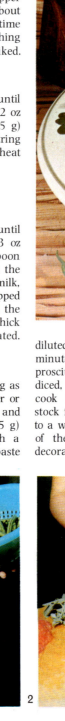

1

2

3

Fennel au Gratin

Ingredients: *4–8 fennel, according to size · 2 oz (60 g) butter or margarine · 2 tablespoons grated Parmesan cheese*

For the béchamel sauce: 2 oz (60 g) butter or margarine · 3 tablespoons flour · 1 pint (½ l) milk · salt · grated nutmeg · 1 tablespoon grated Parmesan cheese · 1 egg yolk · and 2 oz (60 g) cooked ham, diced (optional)

Clean and quarter the fennel (step 1) and parboil it. Drain, and sauté in half the butter or margarine. Prepare the béchamel sauce: melt the butter or margarine in a pan, stir in the flour, cook for 1–2 minutes, remove from the heat and add the cold milk gradually, stirring constantly. Return to the heat and cook for 10 minutes. Remove from the heat, add salt and grated nutmeg to taste, the Parmesan cheese, egg yolk, and ham if using. In a buttered ovenproof dish, arrange the fennel and béchamel sauce in layers (step 2), the fennel with its curved part uppermost. Finish with a light layer of béchamel sauce (step 3), sprinkle with grated Parmesan cheese, dot with remaining butter or margarine, and put in a hot oven (425°F/gas 7) for 20–25 minutes, or until a golden crust has formed on the top. Serve immediately in the cooking dish.

Lima Beans with Salt Pork

Prepare for cooking 2 lb (1 kg) fresh Lima beans – or use frozen beans. In a pan, brown 2 oz (60 g) lard with 6 oz (175 g) salt pork (previously soaked in cold water and cut into slices) and 1 slice of onion, chopped. Add the beans, 2 fl oz (100 ml) stock, salt and pepper to taste and cook over high heat for about 35 minutes or until tender. Serve piping hot in a warm vegetable dish.

Greek Lima Beans

Prepare for cooking 2 lb (1 kg) fresh Lima beans – or use frozen beans. In a pan, brown 1 onion, chopped, with 4 tablespoons oil. Add 1 fennel, cut into strips, sauté for a few minutes, then add the Lima beans. Add 2 fl oz (100 ml) stock, season with salt to taste and cook slowly for about 35 minutes until all the liquid is ab-

sorbed and the beans are tender. Sprinkle with freshly ground pepper, and serve piping hot in a warm vegetable dish.

Haricots Panachés

Cook ½ lb (225 g) fresh haricots in lightly salted boiling water until tender. (Dried haricot beans can be used, in which case, soak them over-

night in cold water, then cook them in plenty of salted water for about 1 hour, until they are tender). In a separate pan, cook ½ lb (225 g) string beans, uncovered, in salted boiling water until tender. When beans are cooked, drain, mix together and sauté lightly in 4 oz (115 g) butter or margarine. Season with salt and pepper to taste. Sprinkle with chopped parsley and serve immediately, piping hot.

Mushroom Caps on Vine Leaves

Ingredients: *4–8 large mushroom caps, according to size · 4–8 vine leaves · a few tablespoons olive oil · salt · pepper · parsley, garlic and oregano to taste, all chopped together*

Clean the mushrooms with a wet cloth (step 1). Make 2–3 incisions in the centre of each cap (step 2). Brush the inside of an ovenproof dish with oil, place the vine leaves at the bottom, put in the mushroom caps (step 3), pour oil over them, sprinkle with salt and pepper to taste, and spread with the parsley, garlic and oregano mixture. Put in a hot oven (425°F/gas 7), and cook for 20 minutes.

Stuffed Mushrooms

Remove the stems of 8 large mushrooms. Clean the caps with a wet cloth. Wash the stems, chop them together with 3 cloves of garlic, 4 oz (115 g) lean salt pork (previously soaked in cold water), and parsley to taste. Add 1 tablespoon breadcrumbs, and season with salt and pepper to taste. Stuff the mushroom caps with this mixture. Brush with olive oil and beaten egg, and cook in the oven for 10–12 minutes until mushrooms are tender. Serve with lemon wedges and parsley sprigs.

Creamed Mushrooms

Clean 1 lb (500 g) mushrooms with a wet cloth. Trim the stems. Sauté lightly in 2 oz (60 g) butter. Add ½ glass port, Madeira or Marsala. Cook over low heat until the wine has almost completely reduced. Add ½ pint (¼ l) single cream. Season with salt and pepper, cover and cook very slowly for 15–20 minutes, or until mushrooms are tender and sauce is reduced.

Mushrooms Bordelaise

Clean 1 lb (500 g) mushrooms with a wet cloth. Remove the stems and chop them together with 4 shallots and 1 clove of garlic. Cut the mushroom caps into large pieces. In a frying pan heat 2 fl oz (50 ml) olive oil. Add the mushroom caps, the stems and the shallots. Season with salt and pepper to taste. When all the mushroom liquid has evaporated, sprinkle with chopped parsley and serve.

Mushroom Pie

Prepare and bake 'blind' pastry in a 10-inch cake tin as above. Meanwhile, clean and slice 1 lb (500 g) fresh mushrooms. Brown lightly ½ onion in 2 oz (60 g) butter or margarine. Remove the onion, put in the mushrooms and sauté lightly. Add 1 small glass flamed brandy (optional) and, after a few minutes, salt and pepper to taste, 1 glass single cream and a few tablespoons béchamel sauce (see p.33). Continue cooking on very low heat for 10 minutes. When the pastry is cooked, remove the paper and beans, fill with the mushroom mixture, sprinkle with grated Parmesan cheese and dot with butter. Return to the oven for 5 minutes to gratiné. Serve immediately, piping hot.

1

2

3

Chef's Salad

*Ingredients: 1 clove of garlic, peeled ·
1 lettuce, washed, drained, dried and broken into
pieces · 2 tomatoes, quartered · 1 small bunch
radishes, sliced · 1 green pepper, cut into strips ·
4 oz (115 g) each cooked ham and chicken, cut
into strips · ½ cucumber, sliced · 2–3 hard-
boiled eggs, quartered · 2 oz (60 g) Gruyère
cheese, cut into strips · 2 celery sticks,
chopped*

*For the dressing: 8–9 tablespoons oil · ½ tea-
spoon Worcestershire sauce · 2–3 tablespoons
vinegar · 1 clove of garlic, halved · salt · pepper*

Prepare the dressing: put all the ingredients
in a screwtop jar with salt and pepper to taste.
Close the jar and shake it well (step 1). Rub
the inside of the salad bowl with the whole
clove of garlic (step 2). Put all the prepared

salad ingredients in the bowl and pour in
prepared dressing, (step 3) removing the halved
garlic cloves. Toss lightly just before serving.

Endive Salad with Salt Pork

Clean, wash, drain, dry and break into pieces
1 lb (500 g) endive. Put in a salad bowl. Sauté
4 oz (115 g) salt pork (previously soaked in
cold water) or bacon, diced, in 1 tablespoon oil
until golden. Drain and add to the endive with
2 hard-boiled eggs, chopped. Pour the fat
remaining in the sauté pan over the salad, add
vinegar to taste, toss lightly and serve immediately. In France this salad is made with dande-
lion leaves.

Caesar's Salad

Rub the inside of the salad bowl with a halved
clove of garlic. Put in 1–2 lettuce hearts –
according to size – washed, drained, dried, and
broken into pieces. Mix 5–6 tablespoons olive
oil in a screwtop jar as above with the juice of
1 lemon, ½ teaspoon mustard powder, salt and
pepper to taste. Just before serving, pour the
dressing over the salad, add 2 egg yolks,
lightly beaten, and mix thoroughly but
carefully. Fry lightly over low heat 2 slices of
bread, diced, in a little oil with 1 clove of
garlic, crushed. Add to the salad, mix quickly –
the bread should remain crisp – and serve
immediately. If a more highly seasoned salad
is preferred, add anchovy fillets, desalted by
soaking in a little milk and cut into pieces,
and Worcestershire sauce.

Mixed Salad

Ingredients: *1 cauliflower · 6 oz (175 g) string beans · 2 hard-boiled eggs · 6 oz (175 g) cooked white chicken meat, cut into strips · 4 oz (115 g) Emmenthal cheese, cut into strips · 2 tomatoes, sliced · mustard powder · vinaigrette dressing (see below) · chopped parsley and basil*

Cook the cauliflower and string beans separately in boiling salted water until *al dente*; drain. Break the cauliflower into flowerets. Separate the whites from the yolks of the hard-boiled eggs, and cut the whites into strips. Put the cauliflower, string beans, chicken, cheese, tomatoes and egg whites in a salad bowl. Mash the egg yolks and blend with mustard powder and vinaigrette dressing to taste. Pour over the salad and toss lightly. Sprinkle with chopped parsley and basil to taste. Serves 6.

Chicory and Beetroot Salad

Trim heads of chicory, and halve lengthwise. Add beetroots, cooked and sliced. Toss in vinaigrette dressing (see below) flavoured with mustard powder to taste.

Country Salad

Mix endive, celery cut into strips, and beetroots, cooked and sliced, and toss in vinaigrette dressing (see below).

Artichoke and Celery Salad

Cut raw artichoke hearts and celery stalks into thin strips. Let stand for a while in cold water and lemon juice. Drain, dry well, and toss in vinaigrette dressing (see below).

Dried Bean Salad

Mix canned or cooked kidney or Lima beans with onion and parsley, chopped. Toss in vinaigrette dressing (see below).

String Bean Salad

Mix string beans, cooked, with 1 teaspoon chopped onion and 1 teaspoon chopped parsley. Toss in vinaigrette dressing (see below).

Tomato Salad

Cut 1 large onion into thin slices. If a mild taste of onion is preferred, soak it in cold water for a little while. Arrange the onion slices at the bottom of a salad bowl. Cover with tomatoes, sliced, sprinkle with chopped parsley, basil, celery and spring onion to taste, pour over vinaigrette dressing (see below), and let stand in refrigerator before serving.

Vinaigrette Dressing

Ingredients: *1 tablespoon vinegar · salt and freshly ground pepper to taste · 3 tablespoons oil*

Put the salt, pepper and vinegar in a bowl. Blend well, add the oil and beat lightly with a fork. The quantity can be altered as necessary, as long as the proportions – 1 part vinegar, 3 parts oil – are the same. To make a large amount, put the ingredients in a screwtop jar or bottle, and shake well. Vinaigrette dressing will keep in the refrigerator for 3–4 days. There are many variations of this basic salad dressing (see the following suggestions).

Garlic dressing (for any salad): let 2 cloves of garlic, peeled, stand in the vinegar for 2–3 days before use.

Tarragon dressing (for any salad): keep a few tarragon twigs in the vinegar bottle.

Mushroom dressing (for green salads): add 4 oz (115 g) raw mushrooms, sliced very thinly.

Roquefort or Gorgonzola cheese dressing (for green salads): add 2 oz (60 g) Roquefort or Gorgonzola cheese, mashed with a fork.

Mustard and anchovy dressing (for potato and cauliflower salads): add 1 teaspoon French mustard powder and 1 teaspoon anchovy paste.

Oil and Lemon Dressing

Proceed exactly as for vinaigrette dressing, but replace the vinegar by lemon juice – in the same proportions. Other ingredients may be added to taste (see the following suggestions).

Caper dressing (for green and fish salads): add 1 teaspoon chopped capers and ½ clove of garlic, mashed.

Lobster roe dressing (for fish salads): add the roe of a cooked lobster, mashed with a fork, ½ tablespoon chopped parsley, and a few drops Worcestershire sauce.

Curry dressing (for green salads): add 1 teaspoon curry powder, and 1 teaspoon chopped shallots or spring onions.

Cooked Vegetable Salad

Ingredients: *1 cauliflower · 1 lb (500 g) carrots · 5 artichokes · ½ lb (225 g) Brussels sprouts · ½ lb (225 g) fresh, frozen or canned green peas, shelled · mayonnaise, commercially prepared or home-made, mixed with chopped parsley and lemon juice to taste*

For the dressing: 1 celery stick · 2 oz (60 g) onion, chopped · oil · vinegar · salt · pepper

Cook the vegetables separately in boiling salted water until *al dente*. Break the cauliflower into flowerets. Cut the carrots into strips (step 1). Discard the outer leaves from the artichokes and quarter them. Combine all the dressing ingredients together and pour over the vegetables in separate dishes (step 2). Let stand for at least 1 hour. Place lettuce leaves on a large round serving dish. Put the peas in the middle, and arrange all the vegetables around, varying the colours as much as possible (step 3). Serve the mayonnaise separately. Serves 6.

Cauliflower Salad

Remove the outer leaves of 1 medium-sized cauliflower and trim the stalk. Wash, and cook in boiling salted water with a slice of lemon and a slice of bread for about 15 minutes until *al dente*. Pass under cold running water, drain, and break into flowerets. Put in a salad bowl with 2 tablespoons capers, 6 anchovy fillets, desalted by soaking in a little milk and chopped, 2 oz (60 g) black olives, pitted and sliced. In a bowl, blend 3 tablespoons oil, 3 tablespoons vinegar (the proportions can be changed according to taste), a few basil leaves and salt and pepper to taste. Pour over the cauliflower, toss lightly, and let stand in a cool place or refrigerator for at least ½ hour before serving.

Potato Salad

Boil, drain and peel 2 lb (1 kg) potatoes. Slice, and put in a salad bowl with just enough cold stock to moisten. Slice 1 onion into very thin rings and add to the bowl. Let stand in a cool place or refrigerator for ½ hour. Pour over vinaigrette dressing (see p.36) before serving, and sprinkle with chopped parsley to taste. Garnish with hard-boiled egg slices, decorated with rolled anchovy fillets (desalted by soaking in a little milk), and tomato quarters.

1   2   3

Stuffed Lettuces

Ingredients: *4 lettuces · 4 oz (115 g) black olives, pitted and cut into thin strips · 2 oz (60 g) anchovy fillets, desalted by soaking in milk and cut into pieces · 2 tablespoons capers · 4 tomatoes (preferably Italian plum type), peeled, seeded and sliced · 2 oz (60 g) pecorino or mozzarella cheese (optional), diced · 1 oz (30 g) butter or margarine · 4 tablespoons oil · salt*

Remove and discard the dark green outer leaves of the lettuces, and wash them thoroughly under cold running water. Blanch in salted water then place upside down to drain on a cloth. When quite dry, insert the olives, anchovies, capers, and cheese if using, between the centre leaves of the lettuces (step 1). Melt the butter or margarine in a pan, remove from the heat and put in the lettuces (step 2). Pour over each 1 tablespoon oil (step 3), sprinkle with salt, cover, and cook for 20–25 minutes over low heat. Transfer to a serving dish and add fresh tomato.

Braised Lettuces

Prepare, blanch and drain 4 lettuces as above. Tie neatly together with string, and place over lettuce 1 onion, sliced, 1 carrot, sliced, 1 celery stick, sliced and 1 clove of garlic, crushed. Dot with 2 oz (60 g) butter and add 1 bouquet garni. Sprinkle with salt, cover with water, and cook until tender, about 25 minutes.

Braised Chicory

With a sharp knife, cut off the hard core from 8 heads of chicory. Remove and discard the yellow outer leaves, and wash thoroughly. Blanch in salted water, then drain and place in an ovenproof dish over a layer of 2 oz (60 g) onions, sliced, and 1 carrot, sliced. Dot with 2 oz (60 g) butter, add 1 bouquet garni, and salt and pepper to taste. Add a little water – not enough to cover the chicory completely – and cook on top of the stove or in a moderate oven.

Chicory au Gratin

Prepare, blanch and drain 8 heads of chicory as above. Put in an ovenproof dish, dot with 2 oz (60 g) butter and pour a little water

around them. Cook on top of the stove or in a moderate oven (375°F/gas 5) for 40–50 minutes or until tender. Meanwhile, prepare a béchamel sauce with 2 oz (60 g) butter, 1 tablespoon flour, and ½ pint (¼ l) milk. Add 3 oz (90 g) grated Gruyère cheese, and salt and grated nutmeg to taste. Pour over chicory, sprinkle with grated cheese and gratiné.

1 2 3

Lentils with Pork

Ingredients: $\frac{3}{4}$ *lb (350 g) dried lentils · 2 oz (60 g) pork fat, chopped · a mixture (to taste) of onion, celery, carrot, parsley, all chopped · 2 oz (60 g) butter or margarine · $\frac{1}{2}$ lb (225 g) canned, peeled tomatoes or 1–2 tablespoons tomato paste · salt · pepper · stock*

To serve: sausages, or duck or pork paupiettes (optional)

Soak the lentils in cold water overnight. Drain (step 1). In a casserole (preferably earthenware) brown the pork fat and the chopped vegetable mixture in the butter or margarine. Add the lentils (step 2), cook for a few minutes then add the tomatoes (step 3) or tomato paste, and salt and pepper to taste.

Cover, and cook very slowly for about $1\frac{1}{2}$ hours, adding hot stock from time to time, until the lentils are tender and the juice is thoroughly reduced. Serve with sausages, duck, or (as in the picture above) pork paupiettes.

Lentils Bordelaise

Soak $\frac{3}{4}$ lb (350 g) dried lentils in cold water overnight. Drain, put in cold water, bring to the boil, skim the scum, add 1 whole onion, peeled and stuck with 2 cloves, 2 tomatoes, peeled, and 1 bouquet garni. Cover, lower the heat and cook slowly for 1 hour. Add $\frac{1}{2}$ pint ($\frac{1}{4}$ l) white wine, 2 cloves of garlic, chopped, and 4 oz (115 g) butter. Season to taste. Cook for a

further 30 minutes, then season with pepper to taste. When lentils are tender, discard onion and bouquet garni, sprinkle with chopped parsley to taste and serve.

Lentil Salad

Soak $\frac{3}{4}$ lb (350 g) dried lentils and drain as above. Put in an earthenware pot with lots of water and a pinch of salt. Bring to the boil, skim off the scum, cook slowly for about $1\frac{1}{2}$ hours until lentils are tender. Rinse under cold running water, drain, and let cool. Toss in vinaigrette dressing (see p.36) and finely chopped garlic and parsley to taste. Let stand for a while in a cool place or refrigerator before serving.

1

2

3

Eggplants Anna

Ingredients: *4—8 round eggplants, according to size · cloves of garlic, thinly sliced · 3 oz (90 g) pecorino or Gruyère cheese, thinly sliced · basil leaves · salt*

For the tomato sauce: 1 slice onion, chopped · 4 fl oz (100 ml) olive oil · 1 lb (500 g) fresh ripe tomatoes, peeled, seeded and quartered · 2 basil leaves · salt · pepper

Remove and discard the stems of the eggplants, wash and dry. Make 3—4 lengthwise incisions in each eggplant (step 1). Insert into each incision 1 slice each of garlic and cheese, and 2 basil leaves rolled in salt (step 2). To make the sauce: brown the onion in the oil, add the tomatoes, basil, and salt and pepper to taste. Bring to the boil, add the eggplants (step 3), cover and cook slowly for about 1 hour, adding stock if necessary. Transfer eggplants to a serving dish and spoon sauce over.

Eggplants with Cheese

Peel 4—8 eggplants, according to size, slice them lengthwise, sprinkle with salt, leave for $\frac{1}{2}$ hour, then pass under cold running water, drain and dry. Brown on both sides, a few at a time, in hot oil; drain. Arrange the slices in a buttered ovenproof dish, alternating layers of eggplant with slices of Emmenthal cheese, a few basil leaves (optional), and freshly ground pepper to taste. Finish with a layer of eggplant, and sprinkle with breadcrumbs and melted butter. Put in a moderate oven (350°F/gas 4), and cook for 25—30 minutes, or until the eggplant is tender and the cheese has melted. Serve in the cooking dish. For an even richer dish, put a few tablespoons béchamel sauce between each layer of eggplant and cheese.

Fried Eggplants

Prepare 4—8 eggplants for cooking as for Eggplants with Cheese, roll in flour, and fry on both sides, a few at a time, in hot oil. Drain and serve immediately.

Eggplants à la Turque

Prepare 4—8 eggplants for cooking as for Eggplants with Cheese, but do not peel them. Roll in flour, and fry on both sides, a few at a time, in hot oil. Drain, sprinkle with salt, and keep warm in a serving dish. Sauté lightly 2 oz (60 g) onion, chopped, in a little of the oil in which the eggplants have been fried. Add 3 cloves of garlic, crushed, 3 tomatoes, peeled and chopped, 1 bay leaf, and salt, pepper, and thyme to taste. Cook slowly for 35 minutes. Add a pinch of cayenne pepper, stir, and pour over the eggplants. Serve hot or cold.

Sicilian Eggplants

Ingredients: *4–8 eggplants, according to size · oil · 2 oz (60 g) grated Parmesan cheese · basil leaves, finely chopped · 1 mozzarella cheese, sliced · 2 tablespoons breadcrumbs*

For the tomato sauce: 1½ lb (750 g) ripe Italian tomatoes, peeled, seeded and chopped, or canned peeled tomatoes, chopped · 1 slice onion, chopped · 1 clove of garlic, crushed · 2 tablespoons oil · 3 basil leaves · salt · pepper

Prepare the tomato sauce: brown the onion and garlic lightly in the oil. Add the tomatoes, basil leaves, salt and pepper to taste, and cook for 30–35 minutes. Work through a sieve. Peel the eggplants, slice them lengthwise, and let stand for ½ hour in cold salted water. Drain, dry thoroughly, and brown on both sides, a few at a time, in hot oil (step 1). Drain, arrange a layer of half the eggplants in a greased ovenproof dish, sprinkle with half the grated Parmesan cheese, basil leaves to taste, and a layer of half the mozzarella cheese. Cover with half the tomato sauce (step 2). Repeat these layers with remaining ingredients (step 3) and top with breadcrumbs. Cook in a hot oven (400°F/gas 6) for ½ hour. Serve hot or cold.

Eggplants Turinois

Prepare 4–8 eggplants for cooking as for Eggplants with Cheese (p.40). Cut 4 cooked ham slices and 8 Emmenthal cheese slices to the same size as the eggplant slices. Put 1 slice ham and 1 slice cheese between 2 slices eggplant, pressing firmly to make them adhere. Roll in flour, dip in 2 eggs beaten with 3 tablespoons milk and a little salt, and fry immediately on both sides, a few at a time, in hot oil. Lift with a slotted spoon, put on paper napkins, and serve piping hot, with a tomato sauce in a separate dish.

Stuffed Eggplants

Halve 4–8 eggplants (according to size) lengthwise. Make criss-cross incisions into the flesh. Sprinkle with salt. Fry, cut side down, in hot oil. Lift with a slotted spoon, remove most of the flesh with a teaspoon (reserving skins), chop and mix with 10 oz (300 g) lean salt pork (previously soaked in cold water for 1 hour).

2 oz (60 g) onion, 2 cloves of garlic, parsley, all finely chopped, and 2 tablespoons breadcrumbs and 1 tablespoon tomato paste. Blend well, season with salt and pepper to taste, and stuff the eggplant skins with this mixture. Brush with olive oil, put in a generously buttered ovenproof dish and bake in a hot oven (400°F/gas 6) for about ½ hour.

Eggplants Provençal

Prepare 4–8 eggplants for cooking as for Eggplants with Cheese (p.40). Roll in flour, and fry on both sides, a few at a time, in hot oil with a mixture (to taste) of garlic and parsley, chopped; drain. Season with salt and pepper to taste and serve immediately.

1

2

3

1

2

3

Glazed Sweet Potatoes

Ingredients: *2 lb (1 kg) medium-sized sweet potatoes · $\frac{1}{2}$ lb (225 g) honey · cinnamon powder or grated lemon peel · 2 oz (60 g) butter or margarine*

Wash the sweet potatoes well, cover with cold salted water, bring to the boil and simmer for about $\frac{1}{2}$ hour until they are *al dente*. Drain, let cool, peel and cut in $\frac{1}{4}$-inch slices (step 1). Arrange the slices in a generously buttered ovenproof dish (step 2). Pour the honey over (step 3), sprinkle with cinnamon or lemon peel to taste, dot with butter or margarine, and bake in a moderate oven (350°F/gas 4) for about $\frac{1}{2}$ hour, basting from time to time with the cooking juices. Serve in the cooking dish at the end of a meal, or as an accompaniment to ham, roast pork, or roast turkey.

Sweet Potato Croquettes

Prepare and cook until *al dente* 2 lb (1 kg) sweet potatoes, as above. Drain, let cool, peel, mash and sieve. In a pan, melt 2 oz (60 g) butter or margarine on low heat, add the sweet potatoes, and cook for a few minutes. Remove from the heat, add salt and grated nutmeg to taste, 1 whole egg, and 1 egg yolk. Blend well, then pour the mixture onto a floured board. Shape into croquettes, dip them into 1 egg white, lightly beaten, then roll in breadcrumbs. Let stand for a while, then fry in hot deep oil until golden. Lift out with a slotted spoon and drain on absorbent paper.

Fried Sweet Potatoes

Prepare and cook until *al dente* 2 lb (1 kg) sweet potatoes as above. Drain, let cool, peel and slice. Fry in hot deep oil. Lift out with a slotted spoon and drain on absorbent paper.

Sweet Potatoes with Rum

Prepare, cook and sieve 2 lb (1 kg) sweet potatoes as for Sweet Potato Croquettes above. Place in a bowl, blend in 2 oz (60 g) butter, softened, 4–5 tablespoons single cream, 4 tablespoons rum, and salt and pepper. Pile the mixture into a buttered overproof dish, pour a few spoonfuls melted butter over, and cook in a very hot oven (450°F/gas 8) until golden.

Potatoes Duchesse

Ingredients: *2 lb (1 kg) potatoes · 4 oz (115 g) butter or margarine · 1 whole egg and 3 egg yolks, lightly beaten together · salt · pepper*

To gratiné: *1 egg, beaten with a little salt*

Peel the potatoes, cut them into pieces and put in a pan. Cover with cold salted water, bring to the boil and simmer until tender, taking care they do not break; drain, put back over the heat, shaking the pan, until the potatoes are dry. Work through a sieve, potato ricer or presse-purée (step 1). Add the butter or margarine (step 2), eggs, and salt and pepper to taste. Beat the mixture until fluffy, and put it in a pastry bag fitted with a large rose tube. Pipe small mounds on a buttered baking sheet (step 3). Brush with beaten egg and gratiné.

If liked, small nests can be piped and filled with vegetables to taste – for example, green peas with ham, etc. Begin by piping the centre, then form flat spirals until the required width is obtained. Pipe layers round the edge (step 4).

Potato Croquettes

Prepare, cook and sieve 2 lb (1 kg) potatoes as above. Put over very low heat, add 2 egg yolks, salt and grated nutmeg to taste, beat well, remove from heat, and leave to cool. If liked, add 2 tablespoons grated Parmesan cheese. Shape into croquettes on a floured board, dip into 1 egg white, lightly beaten, then roll in breadcrumbs. Let stand for a while, then fry in hot deep oil. Lift out with a slotted spoon and drain on absorbent paper.

Mashed Potatoes

Prepare, cook and sieve 2 lb (1 kg) potatoes as above. Add 3 oz (90 g) butter or margarine, and, beating constantly, ½ pint (¼ l) milk, and salt and grated nutmeg to taste. When the mixture is fluffy and smooth, put in a pan over low heat and reheat, stirring constantly.

Potatoes Chantilly

Prepare, cook and sieve 2 lb (1 kg) potatoes as above. Mix with 4 fl oz (100 ml) single cream whisked until stiff with salt and pepper, put in a buttered ovenproof dish, sprinkle with grated Gruyère cheese, and gratiné.

1

2

3

4

Fried Potatoes

Peel 2 lb (1 kg) potatoes, preferably old potatoes, squaring off the ends and sides. Cut into slices $\frac{1}{4}$ inch thick, then into matchsticks $\frac{1}{4}$ inch wide. Soak in cold water until cooking time. Drain, dry thoroughly in a cloth, and put in appropriate frying basket. Cover with the other part of the basket, and plunge into hot deep oil (step 1). When the potatoes are crisp and golden, lift basket out, turn out carefully on absorbent paper, sprinkle with salt and serve immediately. (Creamed or buttered vegetables can also be cooked in the basket in this way.)

Potato Gaufrettes

Prepare and cook 2 lb (1 kg) potatoes as for Potato Chips above, cutting potatoes very thinly with a mandoline (step 2).

Potatoes Pont-Neuf

Peel 2 lb (1 kg) old potatoes, squaring off the ends and sides. Cut into $\frac{1}{2}$-inch thick slices, then into sticks 2 inches or more in length. Soak in cold water until cooking time, drain, dry thoroughly in a cloth, and put, a few at a time, in about 2 quarts (2 l) hot deep oil for 8–10 minutes until golden, shaking the pan from time to time. Between each batch of potatoes, reheat the oil to very hot. Drain the potatoes on absorbent paper, sprinkle with salt and serve.

Straw Potatoes

Proceed as for Potatoes Pont-Neuf, cutting potatoes $\frac{1}{8}$ inch thick. Cook in a frying basket, if available (step 3).

Puffed Potatoes

Peel 2 lb (1 kg) old potatoes, wipe them with a cloth, but do not wash them, and cut them into slices $\frac{1}{4}$ inch thick. Then proceed as for Potatoes Pont-Neuf, cooking the potatoes until lightly coloured in hot oil (350°F), lifting out with a slotted spoon and draining them on absorbent paper, then heating the oil to a higher temperature (400°F), and cooking them again, until they swell up and are golden brown. Lift out with a slotted spoon, drain on absorbent paper, sprinkle with salt and serve.

Potato Chips

Peel 2 lb (1 kg) old potatoes, cut into very thin ($\frac{1}{8}$ inch) slices (step 2), and put in cold water until cooking time. Drain, dry thoroughly in a cloth, and cook in hot deep oil until golden and crisp, shaking the pan from time to time. Lift out with a slotted spoon, put on absorbent paper, sprinkle with salt, and serve immediately.

Potatoes Chasseur

Wash and parboil 2 lb (1 kg) potatoes. Drain, peel, let cool and slice. Brown 4 tablespoons oil with 1 clove of garlic, peeled. Remove garlic, add the potatoes, and when golden add $\frac{1}{2}$ glass dry white wine. Let evaporate, add 1 lb (500 g) canned peeled tomatoes, 1 bay leaf, and salt and pepper. Cover, and cook slowly until potatoes are tender. Remove bay leaf.

1   2   3

1 2 3

Stuffed Potatoes au Gratin

Ingredients: *8 large oval potatoes*

For the stuffing: *2 oz (60 g) butter or margarine · 1 tablespoon flour · ¼ pint (⅛ l) milk · salt · grated nutmeg · 2 oz (60 g) grated cheese · 4 oz (115 g) cooked ham, diced · boiled green peas (optional) · 1 egg yolk*

To garnish: *watercress*

Peel the potatoes and halve them lengthwise. Remove some of the pulp from the centre with a sharp knife (step 1). Trim the bottoms so they can stand upright. Put in cold salted water, bring to the boil and cook for 5 minutes, lift out with a slotted spoon, drain, and let cool on absorbent paper. Meanwhile, prepare a béchamel sauce: melt the butter or margarine in a pan, stir in the flour, cook 1–2 minutes,

remove from the heat and add the cold milk gradually, stirring constantly. Return to the heat and cook for 10 minutes. Remove from the heat, add salt and grated nutmeg to taste, the cheese, ham, peas (if using) and, finally, the egg yolk. Blend well, and fill the potatoes with this mixture (step 2). Arrange in a buttered ovenproof dish (step 3), and bake in a moderate oven (350°F/gas 4) for 30–40 minutes until potatoes are tender. Garnish with watercress.

Potatoes Lyonnaise

Peel 2 lb (1 kg) potatoes, wash, cover with cold salted water, bring to the boil and simmer until tender. Drain, let cool and slice. Meanwhile, blanch 1 large onion, thinly sliced, for a few minutes in boiling water, drain, and dry in a cloth. Sauté lightly in 1 oz (30 g) butter, and

continue cooking slowly. In a large frying pan, brown 2 oz (60 g) butter or margarine, add the potatoes and, when they are golden, add the onion slices. Season to taste, continue cooking for a few minutes over high heat, sprinkle with chopped parsley, and serve.

Potatoes Anna

Peel 2 lb (1 kg) potatoes. Cut into very thin, regular slices. Sauté in 2 oz (60 g) butter in a frying pan, taking care they do not stick together. Butter generously a pastry mould or round ovenproof dish. Sprinkle the potato slices with salt, and arrange in the mould in a spiral pattern. When the bottom is covered, dot with butter, and continue layering, buttering every other layer. Cover, cook in hot oven (400°F/gas 6) for 45 minutes. Unmould.

1

2

3

Stuffed Sweet Peppers

Ingredients: *4 large peppers (preferably red or yellow)*

For the stuffing: *1 large eggplant · 2 celery sticks · 1 small green pepper · 4 oz (115 g) tuna fish in oil · 2 anchovy fillets, desalted by soaking in milk · 4 fl oz (100 ml) oil · 1 clove of garlic · 4 oz (115 g) olives · 1 oz (30 g) capers · 1 tablespoon tomato paste · stock · salt*

Wash the large peppers, cut off tops and remove the seeds and white pith (step 1). Blanch in boiling salted water for 5 minutes then rinse under cold running water; drain well. Prepare the stuffing: peel and dice the eggplant, cut the celery into pieces, remove seeds and pith from the green pepper, and cut into strips (step 2), drain the tuna fish and the anchovy fillets, and chop. In ½ the oil, brown the garlic, then remove and discard it. Add the eggplant, celery, pitted olives and capers, then the tomato paste and a little stock. Season with a little salt, cover, and cook slowly, adding a little more stock occasionally, until vegetables are tender. Remove from the heat and add the vinegar. Stuff the peppers with this mixture (step 3), and place them in a pan, with the remainder of the oil and a little water. Cook in a moderate oven (350°F/gas 4) for about ½ hour, or until peppers are tender.

Peperonata

Prepare 2 lb (1 kg) red and yellow sweet peppers as for Sweet Peppers with Anchovies. Dip 1½ lb (750 g) ripe tomatoes (preferably Italian plum type) in boiling water, peel, seed, and cut into pieces and remove seeds. In a pan, put 4 fl oz (100 ml) oil, the peppers, tomatoes, 1 medium-sized onion, sliced, and a few basil leaves. Cover, and cook over low heat for about 1½ hours. Halfway through the cooking, season with salt to taste. If necessary, add a few spoonfuls of water, or, if there is too much liquid, uncover the pan and reduce over high heat. Serve hot, as an accompaniment to meats (particularly boiled meats) or cold as an hors d'oeuvre.

Sweet Peppers with Anchovies

Wash 2 lb (1 kg) red and yellow sweet peppers, halve, remove the seeds, pith and tops, and cut into wedges. In hot oil soften on low heat 2 oz (60 g) anchovy fillets, desalted by soaking in a little milk and mashed. Add the peppers, a little salt, and cover. Cook slowly for about 1½ hours, stirring occasionally, and adding a few spoonfuls of stock if the peppers become dry. Serve hot or cold.

Green Peas with Lettuce

Ingredients: *4 lettuces · 1 lb (500 g) green peas (shelled) · 4 oz (115 g) small new onions, sliced · 4 oz (115 g) butter or margarine · salt · 3 tablespoons hot stock · chopped parsley · pepper*

Remove and discard the large outer leaves of the lettuces, wash the lettuce thoroughly under running water, and drain. In a large pan, melt ½ the butter or margarine over low heat. Add the peas, the onions (step 1), and the lettuces (step 2). Season with salt to taste, add the stock, cover, and cook slowly for 15–20 minutes. Add parsley and pepper to taste (step 3) butter or margarine and cook until juice is reduced.

Green Peas à la Française

Chop ½ lettuce, washed and drained as above.

Put 1 lb (500 g) green peas in a pan, add 2½ oz (75 g) butter or margarine, 1 tablespoon flour, 4 oz (115 g) onions, sliced and the chopped lettuce. Stir with a wooden spoon, add 3 tablespoons sugar, ½ teaspoon salt, and cover with water. Boil over high heat, uncovered, for 15–20 minutes, until peas are tender and water has been absorbed.

Flemish Green Peas

Scrape and dice 10 oz (300 g) carrots. Put in a pan, cover with water, season with salt, add 2 oz (60 g) butter or margarine and 1 teaspoon sugar. Cook, uncovered, until all the liquid has been absorbed. Meanwhile, in another pan, cook 1 lb (500 g) green peas in boiling salted water — uncovered — for 15–20 minutes or until tender. Drain, and mix with the carrots. Add 2 oz (60 g) butter or margarine, sprinkle

with chopped parsley to taste, stir well and serve.

Green Peas with Salt Pork

Dice 6 oz (750 g) lean salt pork (previously soaked in cold water for ½ hour). Chop finely 2 oz (60 g) onion (or use 4 oz/115 g small onions, whole). Cook 1 lb (500 g) green peas in boiling salted water with a twig of thyme. Brown the onion and the salt pork in 1 oz (30 g) butter or margarine. Cook for a few minutes, then add to the peas. Blend 2 oz (60 g) butter or margarine with 1 tablespoon flour. Add to the peas, and continue cooking until they are tender. Sprinkle with chopped chervil to taste before serving.

1 2 3

Baked Tomatoes Stuffed with Rice

Ingredients: *8 large round, ripe tomatoes · 8 tablespoons rice · 1 clove of garlic · parsley or mint to taste · 3 oz (90 g) butter or margarine · salt · pepper · a few tablespoons tomato paste · stock*

To garnish: *8 mint leaves*

Wash the tomatoes and slice off the top of each (step 1). Remove the pulp with a teaspoon (step 2), seed, squeeze, and reserve, together with the caps. Crush the garlic with the parsley or mint. Mix in a bowl with the rice, 1 oz (30 g) melted butter, 2 tablespoons tomato pulp, salt and pepper to taste. Put a little melted butter or margarine and salt and pepper in each hollowed tomato and on the inside of each cap. Arrange the tomatoes in a generously buttered ovenproof dish. Fill them with the prepared rice mixture (step 3). Cover with the caps, pour around the tomato paste

diluted with stock, and bake in a moderate oven (350°F/gas 4) for 30–35 minutes. Serve in cooking dish, garnishing with mint leaves.

Stuffed Tomatoes

Wash 8 large round, ripe tomatoes and slice off the top of each. Remove the pulp carefully with a teaspoon, and reserve. Season the insides with salt, and keep them upside down on a plate so that the water runs out. In a bowl, mix 1 generous handful of bread, soaked in milk and squeezed, ½ lb (225 g) chopped cooked meat to taste, chopped parsley and onion to taste, 1 egg yolk, a few spoonfuls grated Parmesan cheese, salt and pepper to taste, and enough reserved tomato pulp to obtain a smooth mixture. Dry the tomatoes, stuff with the meat mixture and arrange in a buttered ovenproof dish. Sprinkle with breadcrumbs, dot with butter, and cook in a

moderate oven (350°F/gas 4) for 30–35 minutes until a golden crust has formed on tops of tomatoes. Serve in the cooking dish.

Tomatoes au Gratin

Wash and halve 4 tomatoes. Remove the pulp with a teaspoon as above and reserve. Season the insides with salt, and keep upside down on a plate. In a frying pan, brown 8 tablespoons breadcrumbs in 6 tablespoons hot oil. Remove from the heat, add anchovy paste to taste (or anchovy fillets desalted in milk, drained and mashed) diluted in a little oil, the reserved tomato pulp, chopped parsley, salt and pepper to taste. Dry the tomatoes, stuff with this mixture, and put them in a buttered ovenproof dish. Brush with oil, and cook in a moderate oven (350°F/gas 4) for 30–35 minutes, until a golden crust has formed on the tops of the tomatoes. Serve in the cooking dish.

Leeks with Prosciutto

Ingredients: *2 lb (1 kg) large leeks · 4 oz (115 g) sliced prosciutto or cooked ham · grated Parmesan cheese · 4 oz (115 g) butter or margarine, melted · salt · pepper*

Remove and discard the green part of the leeks (step 1), peel off the thin skin of the white part, and pare the bottoms. Wash thoroughly and cook in boiling salted water for 15–20 minutes until tender. Drain, leave to dry on a napkin, then wrap 2–3 leeks – according to size – in a slice of prosciutto (step 2). Arrange in a buttered ovenproof dish, sprinkle with grated Parmesan cheese, salt and pepper to taste, brush with melted butter or margarine (step 3), and put in a moderate oven (350°F/gas 4) to gratiné. Serve in the cooking dish.

Leeks au Gratin

Prepare 2 lb (1 kg) leeks as above, and cook in boiling salted water for 15–20 minutes until tender. Drain, and cut into short pieces. Meanwhile, prepare a mornay sauce in the following manner: in a pan, melt 2 oz (60 g) butter, stir in 2 oz (60 g) flour, cook for 2 minutes, remove from the heat, and add gradually 1 pint ($\frac{1}{2}$ l) cold milk, stirring constantly. Return to heat, bring to the boil and let simmer for 10 minutes. Remove from the heat, add 1 egg yolk, 5 oz (150 g) grated Parmesan cheese, salt and grated nutmeg to taste. Stir well. In an ovenproof dish, arrange the leeks in a layer, pour the sauce over them, sprinkle with breadcrumbs, dot with butter, and put in a moderate oven (350°F/gas 4) to gratiné. Serve in the cooking dish.

Braised Leeks

Prepare 2 lb (1 kg) leeks as for Leeks with Prosciutto above. Dry thoroughly. Arrange in a buttered ovenproof dish. Cover with a mixture of finely chopped celery, carrot and onion to taste. Add 1 bay leaf, sprinkle with salt and pepper, and cover with stock. Cover the dish, and cook in a moderate oven (350°F/gas 4) for 40–45 minutes, or until the leeks are tender and all the cooking liquid has been absorbed. Serve the dish as it is or add 2 whole eggs beaten with a little milk and a pinch of salt and return to the oven for a few minutes.

Leeks Vinaigrette

Prepare 2 lb (1 kg) leeks as for Leeks with Prosciutto above, taking care to cut all leeks to the same size. Poach in salted water for about 25–30 minutes until tender, but not too soft. Drain, cool, and serve coated in vinaigrette dressing (see p.36) as an hors d'oeuvre.

2

3

1   2   3

Stuffed Turnips

Ingredients: *4 large turnips (or 8 small ones) ·
4 oz (115 g) Emmenthal cheese, sliced · 4 oz
(115 g) prosciutto, sliced · grated Parmesan
cheese · 3 oz (90 g) butter or margarine, melted*

Peel the turnips, wash them, and cook until
al dente (about 15 minutes) in boiling salted
water. Drain, cool, and slice them horizontally
(step 1). Put them back into shape alternating
layers of turnip, cheese and prosciutto (step 2),
and place in a buttered ovenproof dish (step 3).
Sprinkle with grated Parmesan cheese, brush
with melted butter or margarine and put in a
moderate oven (350°F/gas 4) for 20–25
minutes, or until the turnips are cooked and
lightly golden. You can also cover the turnips
with béchamel sauce before putting them in
the oven. Serve in the cooking dish.

Purée Freneuse

Peel and wash 1½ lb (750 g) turnips. Cut into
quarters, and cook in boiling salted water for
15–20 minutes, together with ¾ lb (350 g)
potatoes, peeled and quartered. Drain, work
through a food mill or sieve (or purée in a
blender), put back over the heat, stirring constantly. Add 4 oz (115 g) butter and 4 fl oz
(100 ml) single cream, season with salt and
pepper to taste, and serve in a warm vegetable
dish garnished with croûtons fried in butter.

Turnips au Gratin

Peel and wash 1 lb (500 g) turnips. Cook for
15–20 minutes in boiling salted water until
tender. Drain, cool, and slice. Brown in 1 oz
(30 g) butter or margarine. Put in an ovenproof dish in layers, covering each layer of
turnips with a few tablespoons béchamel sauce
2½ oz (75 g) butter, 3 tablespoons flour, 1 pint
(½ l) milk, salt and grated nutmeg to taste) and
grated Gruyère cheese. End with a layer of
béchamel sauce, sprinkle with breadcrumbs,
dot with butter, and put in a hot oven (400°F/
gas 6) for 10–15 minutes to gratiné.

Sautéed Salsify

Scrape 2 lb (1 kg) white salsify. Cut in pieces,
and put immediately in water mixed with lemon
juice. Cook for about 40 minutes in boiling
salted water until tender. Drain, and sauté in
2 oz (60 g) butter or margarine, with 2 cloves
of garlic. Remove garlic, season and serve.

Neapolitan Ratatouille

Ingredients: *2 large onions · 3 eggplants · 1 lb (500 g) ripe tomatoes (preferably Italian plum type) · 4 zucchini · 4 green peppers · ½ lb (225 g) fresh or canned artichoke hearts, quartered · 4 fl oz (100 ml) oil · 1 or 2 cloves of garlic, peeled · 1 bouquet garni of parsley, 1 bay leaf and thyme · salt · pepper*

Peel and slice the onions, cut the eggplants, tomatoes and zucchini into pieces (step 1), and the green peppers into strips, having removed tops, pith and seeds. In a pan (preferably earthenware) put the oil and the onions, and cook until tender, but not browned. Add the eggplants, zucchini, peppers, tomatoes, the garlic cloves, the bouquet garni, and salt and pepper to taste (step 2). Cover, and cook very slowly for about 1 hour, stirring gently from time to time. If toward the end of the cooking there is too much liquid, raise the heat and remove the cover. A few minutes before the end of the cooking, add the artichoke hearts (step 3). Take out the garlic cloves and bouquet garni. Serve hot or cold.

Artichokes and Potatoes Country Style

Remove the outer leaves and the stems of 4 artichokes, quarter them and put in water mixed with lemon juice. Peel and quarter 3–4 medium-sized potatoes. Sauté in 4 fl oz (100 ml) oil 1 chopped spring onion and 1 clove of garlic. Remove garlic, add the drained artichokes and potatoes, and brown. Add 8 oz (225 g) canned peeled tomatoes cut into pieces, basil leaves, salt and pepper to taste. Cover, and cook slowly for 40–50 minutes, adding stock if necessary.

Ratatouille Niçoise

Peel, seed and cut into pieces 4 large tomatoes. Put in a pan with 2 tablespoons olive oil, 2 twigs fresh thyme (or ½ teaspoon dried thyme), and a few basil leaves (or 1 teaspoon dried basil), 1 bay leaf and 2 teaspoons salt. Let simmer. Meanwhile, peel and slice 2 large onions (preferably Spanish), and sauté them in oil, in a frying pan, with 1 clove of garlic, crushed. Add to the pan in which the tomatoes are simmering, and cover. Wash 2 green peppers, cut off tops, discard seeds and pith and slice flesh. Sauté in oil in the frying pan and add to pan. Cook in the same way 1 large eggplant, cut into ¼-inch slices but not peeled, and put it in turn into the pan. Let the ratatouille simmer for about ½ hour. If there is too much liquid after that time, remove the cover and cook a little longer. Check the seasoning. Add freshly ground pepper and serve. The ratatouille is equally good served cold, and keeps well in the refrigerator.

Mixed Vegetables Irma

Peel 3 potatoes, 3 tomatoes and 3 onions. Wash 3 peppers, preferably red or yellow, cut off tops and discard seeds and pith. Chop, together with 3 zucchini. Put in a pan with olive oil, salt and pepper to taste. Cover and cook over very low heat for 3 hours, adding a little water if necessary.

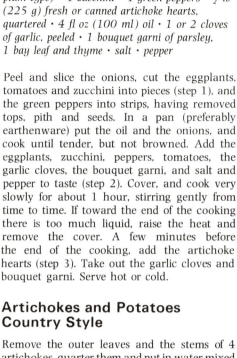

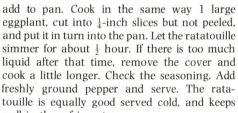

1   2   3

Braised Celery Heads

Ingredients: *2–3 white celery heads ·*
1 onion, sliced · 1 small carrot, sliced ·
2 oz (60 g) beef marrow, sliced · ¼ bay leaf ·
stock · 1 oz (30 g) butter · 1 tablespoon flour ·
salt · pepper

Trim off all leaves and coarse stalks from the
celery (step 1). Wash and halve if small.
Blanch for 5 minutes in boiling salted water
and drain. Place a layer of sliced onion and
carrot at the bottom of a flameproof casserole,
put in the celery heads (step 2), the marrow,
the bay leaf, and cover with stock. Bring to the
boil on top of the stove, then cover the
casserole and put in a moderate oven (350°F/
gas 4) for 1 hour, or until celery is tender. Drain
celery and put it in a buttered ovenproof dish.
Reduce the cooking juices left in the casserole
to 8–10 tablespoons, remove the bay leaf,
add the butter mixed with the flour, season
with salt and pepper to taste, and, as soon as
the sauce has thickened, pour it over the
celery (step 3). Put in a hot oven (425°F/gas 7)
for a few minutes to gratiné.

Celeriac à la Française

Peel 2 large celeriac, dice them and put in cold
water mixed with a little lemon juice. Drain,
dry and sauté for 5 minutes in 1 oz (30 g)
butter or margarine. Cover with stock, cover
the pan and cook until celeriac is tender and
the juices have reduced. Blend in 1 hard-boiled
egg yolk, worked through a sieve, 1 teaspoon
chopped capers, and, little by little, 1 oz (30 g)
butter mixed with 1 tablespoon flour. Stir
carefully so that all the ingredients are
thoroughly blended, and keep over low heat
until a thick sauce is obtained. Check seasoning and pour onto a warm serving dish.

Purée of Celeriac and Potato

Peel and quarter 1 large celeriac, ¾ lb (350 g)
potatoes. Put in cold salted water, bring to
the boil, and cook for about 20 minutes or until
tender. Drain, work through a food mill or
sieve (or purée in a blender). Put back over
low heat, stirring constantly with a wooden
spoon, season with salt and pepper to taste, add
4 oz (115 g) butter and 4 fl oz (100 ml) cream.
Serve in a warm dish, garnished with croûtons.

1   2   3

Artichoke Soufflé

Ingredients: *1 lb (500 g) fresh artichokes · lemon juice · 2 oz (60 g) butter · 2 oz (60 g) flour · ½ pint (¼ l) milk · 1 tablespoon grated Parmesan cheese · salt · nutmeg · 3 eggs · breadcrumbs*

Wash the artichokes, and cook in boiling salted water mixed with a little lemon juice for about 40 minutes. Drain, and work through a food mill (step 1), or sieve. Sauté for 5 minutes in the butter, add the flour, stirring constantly, and finally the milk, little by little (step 2). Continue cooking for about 15 minutes, remove from the heat, and blend in the Parmesan cheese, salt and nutmeg to taste. Pour into a bowl, let cool, then add the eggs, well beaten. Mix thoroughly for 10 minutes (step 3). Butter a soufflé dish (or round mould)

about 7 inches in diameter and 2½ inches deep, sprinkle it with breadcrumbs and pour in the artichoke mixture. Cook in a bain-marie in a moderate oven (350°F/gas 4) for about 30 minutes until set. Unmould on a serving dish and serve immediately. If a golden crust is desired, put in a hot oven (425°F/ gas 7) for a few minutes before serving, and serve in the cooking dish. This soufflé is good eaten with meatballs in tomato sauce, which can be spooned around it on the serving dish.

Carrot Soufflé

Clean, wash and cook 1 lb (500 g) carrots for about 20 minutes in boiling salted water until tender. Drain, and work through a food mill or sieve. Sauté for 5 minutes in 2 oz (60 g) butter,

then add 2 oz (60 g) flour, stirring constantly, and finally, little by little, ½ pint (¼ l) milk. Continue cooking for about 15 minutes. Remove from the heat, and blend in 1 tablespoon grated Parmesan cheese, salt and grated nutmeg to taste. Pour into a bowl and let cool. Add 3 whole eggs, well beaten, and mix thoroughly for 10 minutes. Butter a soufflé dish (or a round mould) about 7 inches in diameter and 2½ inches deep, sprinkle it with breadcrumbs, and pour in the carrot mixture. Cook in bain-marie in a moderate oven (350°F/ gas 4) for about 30 minutes until set, unmould on a warm serving dish and serve immediately. The soufflé can be served in the cooking dish, after putting it in a hot oven (425°F/gas 7) for a few minutes, so that a golden crust forms on the surface.

Spinach Gourmet

Ingredients: $1\frac{1}{2}$ lb (750 g) spinach · 1 handful white bread soaked in milk and squeezed · 2 oz (60 g) tuna fish packed in oil, drained · 2 anchovy fillets, desalted by soaking in a little milk · 2 eggs · 4 tablespoons grated Parmesan cheese · 4 tablespoons breadcrumbs · salt · pepper

To garnish: *mayonnaise · lemon slices · pieces of sweet red pepper*

Clean and wash the spinach, removing hard stems and damaged leaves. Drain and cook for 10 minutes without water. Squeeze and put through a food mill or sieve (or purée in a blender) together with the bread (step 1). Mix with the chopped tuna fish and anchovy fillets, the eggs, Parmesan cheese, breadcrumbs, and salt and pepper to taste. Shape the mixture into a long roll, wrap it in a wet gauze or cheesecloth (step 2), and tie at both ends. Place in a flameproof casserole (step 3), cover with cold salted water, bring to the boil, and simmer gently for about 45 minutes. Drain, let stand for 15 minutes, then remove the gauze. Serve cold, the slices garnished with mayonnaise, and the dish decorated with half slices of lemon topped with pieces of red pepper.

This dish and the following dishes may be made with frozen spinach. Use 1 lb (500 g) frozen spinach and follow cooking instructions on package.

Spinach Croquettes

Clean, cook and purée $1\frac{1}{2}$ lb (750 g) spinach as above. Sauté lightly in butter over moderate heat. Prepare a béchamel sauce with 2 oz (60 g) butter or margarine, 2 oz (60 g) flour, $\frac{1}{2}$ pint ($\frac{1}{4}$ l) milk, and salt, pepper and grated nutmeg to taste. When sauce is lukewarm, add the spinach mixed with 2 eggs and 4 oz (115 g) grated Gruyère cheese. Cook the mixture, one tablespoon at a time, in hot deep oil. Lift out the croquettes with a slotted spoon, drain them on absorbent paper, and serve immediately, piping hot.

Creamed Spinach

Prepare $1\frac{1}{2}$ lb (750 g) spinach for cooking as above. Cook uncovered in boiling salted water

for 5 minutes until tender. Drain, press to remove moisture, and work through a food mill or sieve (or purée in a blender). Prepare a sauce in the following way: melt in a pan 2 oz (60 g) butter, stir in 1 tablespoon flour, cook for 2 minutes, then add spinach and $\frac{1}{2}$ pint ($\frac{1}{4}$ l) single cream, stirring constantly. Season with salt and grated nutmeg to taste. Serve immediately.

Spinach à l'Anglaise

Prepare $1\frac{1}{2}$ lb (750 g) spinach, cook, drain and purée as for Creamed Spinach above. Put in a pan with 3 oz (90 g) butter. When the butter is golden-brown lift out the spinach with a fork. Serve immediately in a warm vegetable dish, with 4 fl oz (100 ml) double cream poured around, and croûtons fried in butter.

1

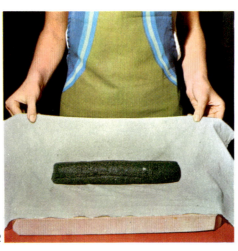

2

3

Jerusalem Artichoke Fritters

Ingredients: *1½ lb (750 g) Jerusalem artichokes*

For the batter: *4 tablespoons flour · salt · 3 tablespoons dry white wine · 1 oz (30 g) butter or margarine, melted · 1 or 2 egg whites*

To garnish: *sprigs of parsley*

Prepare the batter: in a bowl, sieve the flour and the salt, and stir in the white wine and the butter or margarine. Let stand for 1 hour. Meanwhile, scrape the Jerusalem artichokes, wash them, and cook for about 15 minutes in boiling salted water until tender. Drain, let cool, then cut into ¼-inch slices (step 1). Whisk the egg whites until stiff then fold into the batter. Dip the artichokes, a few at a time, into the batter (step 2), and fry them in hot oil (step 3). Lift them out with a slotted spoon when golden, drain on absorbent paper, and serve immediately in a warm vegetable dish garnished with sprigs of parsley.

Jerusalem Artichokes Provençal

Scrape, wash and slice 1½ lb (750 g) Jerusalem artichokes. Heat 4 fl oz (100 ml) olive oil in a frying pan. Add the Jerusalem artichokes and sauté until tender, Season to taste. A few minutes before serving, add a persillade of chopped parsley and 4 cloves of garlic and mix well.

Purée of Jerusalem Artichokes

Scrape and wash 1½ lb (750 g) Jerusalem artichokes. Cook in salted boiling water, together with ½ lb (225 g) potatoes, peeled and washed, for about 15 minutes until both are tender. Drain well and work through a food mill or sieve (or purée in a blender). Put the purée over the heat and let it dry, stirring constantly. Add 4 oz (115 g) butter, season to taste, and add ½ pint (¼ l) single cream. Stir. Serve in a warm dish, garnished with croûtons fried in butter.

Barquettes of Cucumber

Halve two large cucumbers lengthwise, then cut each piece in half across. Carefully remove the seeds and flesh with a teaspoon without

damaging the shell. Dice the flesh. Put in a pan with 2 oz (60 g) butter, paprika and salt to taste. Cover with water, and cook until all the water has evaporated. Add 8 fl oz (200 ml) single cream. Stir well.

Meanwhile blanch the barquettes in boiling salted water. Drain, fill with the diced flesh, and serve immediately.

Creamed Cucumbers

Pare 2 cucumbers – about 1½ lb (750 g) – in the shape of large olives. Put in a pan with 2 oz (60 g) butter and a pinch of salt, and cover with water. Cook uncovered until all the water has evaporated. Add 8 fl oz (200 ml) single cream, cook for a few more minutes, and serve.

Piedmontese Salad

Ingredients: ½ lb (225 g) boiled artichoke hearts · ½ lb (225 g) boiled asparagus tips · 6 oz (175 g) mushroom caps · 1 white truffle · lettuce

For the dressing: *salt · pepper · 2 tablespoons lemon juice · 4 tablespoons oil*

Slice the artichoke hearts (step 1), and cut the asparagus tips into small pieces. Cut the mushroom caps into very thin slices. Arrange in small separate piles in a serving dish. Garnish the edges of the dish with lettuce leaves (step 2). Scrape, wash and dry the truffle, and slice very thinly over the other vegetables (step 3). Prepare the dressing, mixing first the salt and pepper in the lemon juice, then adding the oil. Serve the dressing separately.

Truffles in Mushroom Caps

Clean 8 mushroom caps, and cook them for 3–4 minutes in boiling salted water with a little lemon juice and 1 oz (30 g) butter, or use them raw, if they are fresh. Scrape, wash and dry 1 medium-sized white truffle. Slice it very thinly, and sprinkle with oil, lemon juice and freshly ground pepper. Divide truffle between mushroom caps. Arrange on a serving dish garnished with parsley and wedges of lemon.

Truffles Baked in Ashes

Scrape, wash and dry 4 black truffles. Soak them in brandy for 2 hours. Put 4 slices of pâté de foie gras over 4 slices of salt pork (previously soaked in cold water for ½ hour),

each large enough to enclose 1 truffle. Put 1 truffle over each. Roll shortcrust dough into squares big enough to enclose salt pork, foie gras and truffle. Wrap truffles, sealing pastry edges with water and wrap in a triple thickness of wax paper. Put under ashes covered with hot coals for at least 30 minutes. If ashes are not available, cook them in a moderate oven (350°F/gas 4) for 30 minutes.

Truffles in White Wine

Scrape, wash and dry 4 small black truffles. Put in a pan with 1 glass dry white wine, a pinch of salt, and a little freshly ground pepper. Cover the pan so it is airtight, and cook over high heat for about 10 minutes, or until the wine has completely evaporated.

1   2   3

1   2   3

Breaded Pumpkin

Ingredients: *2 lb (1 kg) pumpkin · 1 egg · salt ·
breadcrumbs · 3 oz (90 g) butter or
margarine · pepper · sliced Emmenthal cheese*

To garnish: *sprigs of parsley*

Remove the rind from the pumpkin, the seeds
and filaments. Cut into ¾-inch thick slices
(step 1). Dip in the egg, beaten with a pinch
of salt, then roll in breadcrumbs (step 2). Let
stand in a cool place for ½ hour. Brown lightly
on both sides in the butter or margarine, and
continue cooking without letting the slices
overlap, until pumpkin is tender. Season with
salt and pepper to taste. Cut the cheese into
small circles if liked, and place on each
pumpkin slice on a flameproof serving dish

(step 3). Cover, and keep over low heat until
the cheese has melted, or put in a hot oven
(425°F/gas 7) for a few minutes. Garnish the
edges of the platter with sprigs of parsley and
serve immediately.

Pumpkin au Gratin

Prepare and cook 2 lb (1 kg) pumpkin as for
Creamed Pumpkin above. Drain, slice, and
arrange the slices in a buttered ovenproof dish.
Sprinkle with pepper, a generous amount of
grated Parmesan cheese, and 2 oz (60 g)
melted butter. Put in a moderate oven (350°F/
gas 4), and bake for about 50 minutes. Serve in
the same dish. If the pumpkin gets too dry
while cooking, add some milk or cream.

Creamed Pumpkin

Prepare 2 lb (1 kg) pumpkin as above. Cut into
pieces, and cook in a little boiling salted water
for 12–15 minutes until tender. Drain, and
mash with a fork. Put back over the heat with
2 oz (60 g) butter or margarine, and, stirring
constantly, let dry completely. Remove from
heat and let cool. Meanwhile, in a bowl, mix
2 tablespoons flour and 4 tablespoons single
cream (or milk). Add 3 eggs, and whip until
fluffy. Add 2 oz (60 g) grated Parmesan cheese,
and salt and grated nutmeg to taste, and blend
into the mashed pumpkin. Pour the mixture
into an ovenproof dish, and cook in a moderate
oven (350°F/gas 4) for 25–30 minutes. Serve
immediately in the cooking dish.

Marinated Zucchini

Ingredients: $1\frac{1}{2}$ lb (750 g) zucchini · oil for frying

For the marinade: $\frac{1}{2}$ onion · 3–4 cloves of garlic · sage leaves · $\frac{1}{2}$ pint ($\frac{1}{4}$ l) vinegar · salt

Wash the zucchini, dry and slice lengthwise. Fry the slices a few at a time in oil (step 1). Lift them out with a spatula and drain on absorbent paper. Arrange on a dish. Fry the onion and garlic, both finely chopped, in hot oil. Add the sage, the vinegar (step 2) and the salt. Boil for a few minutes, pour over the zucchini (step 3), cover, and let marinate for at least 24 hours. Serve cold.

Stuffed Zucchini

Wash and dry 8 small zucchini or 4 large ones. Halve lengthwise. Remove most of the flesh carefully with a teaspoon, without damaging the shell, and reserve. Parboil the shells in boiling salted water to cover. Meanwhile, chop the reserved flesh, and mix with $\frac{1}{2}$ lb (225 g) chopped cooked meat. (Leftovers are ideal, especially lamb.) Cook the mixture in 3 oz (90 g) butter or margarine for 15 minutes, then add 4 oz (115 g) breadcrumbs, and continue cooking for a few more minutes. Remove from the heat, add 2 oz (60 g) grated Parmesan cheese. 1–2 whole eggs, and salt and pepper. Blend well. Drain the zucchini shells, put in a buttered ovenproof dish, fill with prepared stuffing, sprinkle with grated Parmesan cheese, dot with butter, and bake in a moderate oven (350°F/gas 4) for 25–30 minutes. Serve as soon as a golden crust has formed on the surface.

Zucchini with Green Sauce

Wash and dry $1\frac{1}{2}$ lb (750 g) zucchini. Cut into slices (crosswise or lengthwise) and fry, a few at a time, in hot oil. Take out with a slotted spoon and drain on absorbent paper. Prepare a green sauce: chop a generous handful of parsley with 1 clove of garlic and 4 anchovy fillets (previously desalted by soaking in a little milk). Blend in enough oil and vinegar to obtain a smooth, fluid mixture. Season with salt and pepper to taste. Arrange the zucchini in layers in a dish, alternating with layers of green sauce and ending with the latter. Let stand for a few hours before serving.

Zucchini with White Wine

Wash and dry $1\frac{1}{2}$ lb (750 g) zucchini. Cut lengthwise in 4, then cut into squares. In a frying pan cook until golden 1 chopped spring onion in 2 oz (60 g) butter or margarine. Add the zucchini and cook over high heat for 10 minutes. Add $\frac{1}{2}$ glass dry white wine and salt and pepper, cover, lower the heat, and continue cooking, stirring occasionally, until the zucchini are very tender and the cooking juices have reduced. Toward the end of the cooking, raise the heat again to make the zucchini crisp. Just before serving, stir in 2 oz (60 g) diced cooked ham and 1 oz (30 g) butter or margarine. Sprinkle with grated Parmesan cheese.

1

2

3

Preserves

Spiced Herb Vinegar

Ingredients: *1 quart (1 l) red wine vinegar · 2 oz (60 g) fresh rosemary · 4 oz (115 g) fresh mint leaves · 10 fresh sage leaves · 2 small bay leaves · 2–3 cloves of garlic, peeled · 2 teaspoons salt · ¼ oz (7 g) each of cinnamon sticks, whole cloves, peppercorns and mustard seeds*

In an earthenware jar, put all the dry ingredients (step 1). Pour in the vinegar (step 2), then cover the jar with a triple thickness of wax paper and tie securely. Keep in a cool place for at least 15 days, rotating the jar gently every day. Strain the vinegar first through a sieve, then through a paper filter or wet gauze or cheesecloth. Remove the garlic. Pour the vinegar into small sterilized bottles, which will be easier for everyday use, and seal them with corks (or use screwtop jars).

Garlic Vinegar

In a mortar, preferably of marble, mash 4 cloves of garlic with a wooden pestle. Add ½ pint (¼ l) red wine vinegar, and stir for a few minutes. Pour into a 1-quart (1-l) jar, add 1½ pints (¾ l) vinegar, and stir again. Close the jar tightly and keep in a cool dark place for 2–3 days, before straining and bottling the vinegar as above.

Basil Vinegar

Bring to the boil in an earthenware or enamel pan 1 quart (1 l) red wine vinegar. Add 1 generous handful of fresh basil leaves, cleaned with a cloth but not washed, and turn off the heat immediately. (If fresh basil is not available, use 3 tablespoons dried basil.) Cover the pan tightly and let stand for at least 48 hours, before straining and bottling the vinegar as above.

Mint Vinegar

Proceed as for Basil Vinegar above, but using 2 generous handfuls of fresh mint leaves to to 1 quart (1 l) white wine vinegar. Strain bottle and leave to stand for a few weeks before using the vinegar.

Tarragon Vinegar

Bottle about 2 oz (60 g) fresh twigs of tarragon in 1 quart (1 l) red wine vinegar. Seal and let stand for about 48 hours before using the vinegar: there is no need to strain it. You may do the same, in the same proportions, with white wine vinegar.

1

2

Pickled String Beans

Ingredients: *2 lb (1 kg) young fresh string beans · water · rock salt · white vinegar · ¼ oz (7 g) each of cinnamon, whole cloves, mace and peppercorns to each quart (litre) of vinegar*

Wash the string beans, and put them in a bowl. Bring to the boil enough water to cover the beans with 3 tablespoons rock salt to each quart (litre) of water. Let cool, and pour over the beans. Let stand for 24 hours. Meanwhile, in an earthenware or enamel pan bring to a boil enough white vinegar to cover the beans, with ¼ oz (7 g) of each of the spices to each quart (litre), cover, turn off the heat, and leave to infuse for 2–3 hours. Strain through a gauze or cheesecloth. Drain the beans, rinse under cold running water and drain again. Dry thoroughly. Arrange in sterilized jars (step 1) and pour over the cold vinegar to cover (step 2). Seal the jars, and let stand in a cool dark place at constant temperature, wrapping jars in a cloth to protect from sunlight if necessary (step 3), for at least 2 months before using.

Pickled Onions

Ingredients: *2 lb (1 kg) small white pickling onions · 1 quart (1 l) white vinegar · 1 clove of garlic, peeled · 2 whole cloves · 8 peppercorns · 2 bay leaves · 1 cinnamon stick · fresh thyme (optional) · 1 tablespoon rock salt · oil*

Dip the onions in boiling water, cool and peel. Put the garlic, cloves, peppercorns, bay leaves, cinnamon, thyme (if using) and salt in a small muslin bag. Put it with the vinegar in a large earthenware or enamel pan, and bring to the boil. Add the onions, continue boiling for 5 minutes, then drain the onions, reserving the vinegar and discarding the bag. Pack the onions tightly in sterilized jars. Bring the vinegar again to the boil, remove from heat, let cool, and pour over onions to cover. Add 1 bay leaf to each jar, and a layer of oil. Seal and keep as above for 2–3 weeks before using.

Pickled Hot Peppers

Clean with a wet cloth 4 lb (2 kg) hot green peppers, and remove the stems. Place in a very low oven for a few hours to dry out completely. Pack them fairly tightly in warm sterilized

earthenware jars, cover with boiling vinegar, add 1 handful rock salt to each jar, and seal with cork or stopper. After 30 days, drain off the vinegar, cover with fresh vinegar, and add a few cloves of garlic, peeled and blanched.

Pickled Gherkins

Put 4 lb (2 kg) gherkins – about 2 inches long – in a napkin with 4 tablespoons rock salt and shake well, holding the napkin by its corners. Rub them one by one with a cloth or a soft brush. Arrange them in an earthenware or enamel bowl, mix with 1 lb (500 g) rock salt and let stand 6–7 hours to make them lose their water. Remove and dry one by one. Put in sterilized glass jars together with 4 cloves of garlic, peeled and blanched, and 3 hot red peppers. Cover with vinegar, and seal the jars. Keep as above, changing the vinegar after 1 month.

1

2

3

1 2 3

Preserved Mixed Vegetables

Ingredients: *1 cauliflower · 4 carrots · 4 celery sticks · 2 green peppers · ½ lb (225 g) red and yellow peppers · 4 oz (115 g) olives · 1 quart (1 l) white vinegar · ½ pint (¼ l) olive oil · 4 oz (115 g) sugar · 2 teaspoons salt · ½ teaspoon pepper · 1 teaspoon oregano*

Slice cauliflower flowerets, scrape carrots and cut into sticks, cut the celery into pieces, discard tops, seeds and white pith from the peppers and cut flesh into strips; leave olives whole. In a large earthenware or enamel pan, put the washed and dried vegetables, the vinegar, oil, sugar, salt, pepper and oregano (steps 1 and 2). Bring to the boil, stirring from time to time, cover, and cook slowly for 5 minutes. Turn off the heat, leave to cool, then put the vegetables together with the cooking liquid in sterilized jars (step 3). Seal, and let stand in a cool dark place at constant temperature for at least 2 months before using.

Pickled Mushrooms

Put 3 blades of mace and ½ oz (15 g) peppercorns in a muslin bag and put in an earthenware or enamel pan together with 1 quart (1 l) vinegar. Bring to the boil, cover, turn off the heat, and leave to infuse for 2–3 hours. Strain. Peel and trim fresh mushrooms, put in a pan, sprinkle lightly with salt, and cook gently until juice flows. Continue cooking until juice has evaporated. Cover with the spiced vinegar and simmer for 2–3 minutes. Let cool. Pour into sterilized jars, seal, and keep as above.

Pickled Eggplants

Remove stems and green parts of medium-sized eggplants. Slice them lengthwise, without peeling, and put in an earthenware or enamel pan. Cover with water, add a generous amount of salt, and let stand for 24 hours.

Meanwhile, bring to the boil enough vinegar to cover the eggplants with 1 oz (30 g) each of garlic basil, or mint leaves, parsley and peppercorns in a muslin bag. Cover, turn off heat, and leave for 2–3 hours. Strain. Drain the eggplants, rinse, drain again, and dry well. Pack in sterilized jars with the cold vinegar, seal, and keep as above.

Pickled Sweet Peppers

Remove tops from 7 lb (3 kg) yellow and red sweet peppers and cut peppers into wedges: 6 wedges to each pepper. Discard the seeds and white pith. Wipe with a wet cloth. Put in an earthenware or enamel pan together with 1 quart (1 l) white vinegar, ½ pint (¼ l) olive oil, and 1 tablespoon salt. Bring to the boil, and cook for 3 minutes. Remove from the heat, let cool, and put the peppers with the cooking liquid in sterilized jars. Seal, and keep as above.

1   2   3

Chow Chow

Ingredients: *2 quarts (2 l) water · 6 oz (175 g) rock salt · ½ lb (225 g) each of quartered green tomatoes, small cucumbers, whole or halved, chopped gherkins, whole small white pickling onions, chopped celery, string beans, cut into pieces, cauliflower flowerets, cut into pieces, chopped green peppers · 1½ pints (¾ l) white vinegar · 4 oz (115 g) sugar · 2 tablespoons flour · ½ teaspoon turmeric · 2 tablespoons mustard*

Boil water with salt. When cold, pour over prepared vegetables. Let stand for at least 12 hours. Drain, rinse vegetables under running water, drain again. Put in an earthenware or enamel pan, add vinegar, and bring slowly to the boil. In a bowl, mix the sugar with the flour, the turmeric, the mustard, and enough vinegar from the pan to obtain a smooth paste (step 1). Add to the vegetables (step 2), and continue cooking over moderate heat for 5–6 minutes, stirring constantly. Pour immediately into 1-pint (½-l) warm sterilized jars, filling them up to the top (step 3). Seal, and keep in a cool dark place at constant temperature.

Prune Chutney

Pit and slice in four 3 lb (1½ kg) prunes. Peel 1 lb (500 g) apples, remove the cores, and chop finely. Chop 10 oz (300 g) onions. Mix in a bowl with 1 lb (500 g) small grapes. In an earthenware or enamel pan, bring to the boil 1 quart (1 l) white vinegar, with 1 lb (500 g) sugar, 1 teaspoon powdered cloves, 1 teaspoon powdered cinnamon, 1 teaspoon ground ginger, 1 teaspoon mixed spice, and 2 tablespoons salt. Add the fruit and the onion, and cook very slowly, stirring from time to time, until a well blended, thick mixture is obtained. Pour the chutney immediately into 3 warm sterilized 1-pint (½-l) jars. Seal, and keep in a cool dark place at constant temperature. For a sharper taste, add chilli powder.

Pickled Walnuts

Select 50 fresh (green) walnuts and prick them with a needle to make sure they are not hard. Boil enough water to cover walnuts with 1 tablespoon rock salt for each quart (litre) water. Pour over the walnuts. Let stand for 10 days, changing the salted water every 3 days. After that time, drain the nuts, dry them with a cloth, and prick them repeatedly with a large needle. In a bowl, mix 3 tablespoons fresh root ginger, or ground ginger, 2 tablespoons peppercorns, 2 tablespoons mixed spice, 1 tablespoon whole cloves, 1 tablespoon mustard seeds, and ½ tablespoon grated nutmeg. Put the walnuts in warm sterilized jars, alternating with layers of spices, and fill the jars with cider vinegar boiled for 4–5 minutes. Seal and keep as above for at least 2 months.

Sweet-and-Sour Olives

Wash, drain and dry 1 lb (500 g) green or black olives. Put the olives in ½- or 1-pint (¼-½ l) warm sterilized jars. In an earthenware or enamel pan, put 2 oz (60 g) sugar, 4 tablespoons rock salt, 4 tablespoons mustard seed, 1 quart (1 l) white vinegar, and ½ pint (¼ l) water. Bring to the boil, and cook for 4 minutes. Pour immediately over the olives, and seal the jars. Keep as above for at least 15 days before using.

Cheese

Mozzarella Cartwheels

Ingredients: *8 slices white bread · 1–2 mozzarella cheeses · 2 eggs · 2 tablespoons milk · salt · oil or pork fat · pepper*

Cut the bread slices into rounds. Put on each 1 slice mozzarella cheese (step 1). Roll in flour, dip in the egg beaten with the milk and a pinch of salt (step 2), and fry in hot oil or fat until golden (step 3). Remove from pan, drain on absorbent paper and sprinkle with pepper.

Gorgonzola Cheese Balls

Mash with a fork ½ lb (225 g) gorgonzola cheese, softened with a little cream. Add 1 tablespoon grated onion, 1 tablespoon chopped parsley and 2–3 pickled gherkins, finely chopped. Mix well and shape into balls with the hands. Roll the balls in almonds, peeled, grilled, finely chopped, and mixed with paprika to taste. Keep in the refrigerator for a few hours, and serve as an appetizer.

Fried Mozzarella

Cut 2 mozzarella cheeses into slices. Roll in flour, dip in egg beaten with a pinch each of salt and pepper, and finally roll in breadcrumbs. Dip once more in the egg, and in the bread-crumbs. Let stand in the refrigerator for ½ hour, then fry, a few slices at a time, in hot deep oil. Lift out with a slotted spoon, drain on absorbent paper, and serve piping hot, with a tomato sauce in a separate dish if liked.

Croque-Monsieur

Butter 4 slices of white bread. Place on each slice 1 thin slice of Gruyère cheese, ½ slice cooked ham, another slice Gruyère cheese, and 1 slice of bread. Butter the outsides of the bread. Place on a metal plate or baking sheet, sprinkle with grated Gruyère cheese, and put in a moderate oven (350°F gas 4) until the bread is golden on both sides and the cheese begins to melt. You can also fry the croque-monsieur in butter in a frying pan. Serve as an entrée, or, cut in four, as a cocktail appetizer.

Croque-Madame

Proceed exactly as for the croque-monsieur, using cooked white chicken meat, cut into strips, instead of ham.

Fried Cheese Balls

Whip 2 egg whites with a pinch each of salt and paprika until stiff. Blend with 2 oz (60 g) grated Parmesan cheese. Cook the mixture, 1 spoonful at a time, in hot deep oil. Lift out the balls with a slotted spoon when golden, and drain on absorbent paper. Sprinkle with paprika.

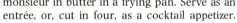

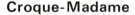

1   2   3

Quiche Lorraine

Ingredients: for the pastry, *6 oz (175 g) flour · 1 pinch salt · 3 oz (90 g) butter · 3 tablespoons water*

For the filling: *6 slices bacon · 8 slices Emmenthal cheese · 4 eggs · ½ pint (¼ l) single cream · grated nutmeg · salt · pepper*

To prepare the pastry, sift the flour with the salt onto a pastry board or a table top. Put the butter, cut into small pieces, in the centre, and gradually draw in the flour with the tips of the fingers until the mixture resembles fine breadcrumbs. Add the water quickly, and knead the dough into a ball. Wrap in wax paper, and let stand in a cool place or refrigerator for at least 20 minutes. Then roll out the dough with a rolling pin to a ¼-inch thickness, and line with it a buttered shallow cake tin, about 8–10 inches in diameter, forming a pinched edge all around (step 1). Prick the dough with a fork and leave to relax. Meanwhile, fry the bacon in a frying pan until crisp, drain, and arrange on the dough. Cover with the Emmenthal cheese (step 2). Beat the eggs with the cream, and nutmeg, salt and pepper to taste, and spoon over the cheese (step 3). Put the quiche in a moderate oven (350°F/gas 4) for about 40 minutes until set and golden.

Camembert en Surprise

Place a whole Camembert cheese in a deep dish, and cover with dry white wine. Let stand for 12 hours, then scrape off the surface of the cheese, and mash the pulp together with 4 oz (115 g) fresh softened butter. Mix well and reshape the cheese in its original form. Roll it in almonds or hazelnuts, toasted and finely chopped, and let stand in the refrigerator for a few hours. Take out ½ hour before serving. Serve at the end of a meal with hot toast.

Welsh Rarebit

In a bowl mix 1 tablespoon mustard powder, 1 pinch each of salt and cayenne pepper, 1½ teaspoons Worcestershire sauce, and 1 tablespoon beer. Put in a double boiler 1 lb (500 g) grated Cheddar cheese and 1 oz (30 g) butter. Stir with a wooden spoon while the cheese begins to melt, and add gradually 12 tablespoons beer opened a few hours before. Add the Worcestershire sauce mixture, and finally 1 egg, beating vigorously until all the ingredients are well blended. Serve on hot buttered toast.

1

2

3